UNION-CASTLE LINERS

FROM GREAT BRITAIN TO AFRICA 1946–1977

WILLIAM H. MILLER

AMBERLEY PUBLISHING

ACKNOWLEDGEMENTS

Like the staff of a Union-Castle liner, many hands were involved in the creation of this book. The idea actually sprang up during a meeting with Campbell McCutcheon in January 2012. And so, appreciation to Campbell for seeing it through and to Amberley, and to Louis Archard, for creating another fine book. High thanks also to Robert Lloyd for his superb covers and to David Williams for his thoughtful and evocative Foreword. My dear friend and superb collector Albert Wilhelmi was a huge resource for photos.

Other materials, from recollections to photos to memorabilia, came from others and so very special thanks to all of them - Jim Alford, the late Frank Andrews, Harry Andrews, Ernest Arroyo, Stephen Card, John Castlemere, Luis Miguel Correia, the late Bob Cummins, Charles and Jean Darnell, the late Alex Duncan, Richard Faber, Howard Franklin, the late John Gillespie, Harry Gunston, Andrew Kilk, the late John Havers, Andy Hernandez, Mike Howe, David Hutchings, Norman Knebel, Peter Knego, Mick Lindsay, John & Sue Mengers, Robert Pabst, Michael Stephen Peters, Dorothy Reminick, Peter Rushton, the late L. A. Sawyer, the late Antonio Scrimali, Roger Sherlock, Steffen Weirauch, Kenneth Wrightman and Victor Young.

Organizations that have assisted include Southern Newspapers Ltd, the Steamship Historical Society of America, Union-Castle Line and the World Ship Society.

If anyone has been omitted, my sincere apologies.

To the officers, staff, crew and of course the passengers who altogether created the great Union-Castle Line

First published 2013

Amberley Publishing Plc
The Hill, Stroud
Gloucestershire, GL5 4EP

www.amberley-books.com

Copyright © William H. Miller, 2013

The right of William H. Miller to be identified as the Author of this work has been asserted in accordance with the Copyrights, Designs and Patents Act 1988.

ISBN 978 1 4456 0956 0

British Library Cataloguing in Publication Data.
A catalogue record for this book is available from the British Library.

Typeset in 10pt on 13pt Celeste.
Typesetting by Amberley Publishing.
Printed in the UK.

CONTENTS

FOREWORD   5

INTRODUCTION   7

EARLY CASTLE LINERS   9

AFTERWORD   126

BIBLIOGRAHY   128

FOREWORD

Of all the great British shipping companies, Union-Castle Line, long associated with Southampton and London, was one of the greatest. Its origins were in the Union Line established in 1855 and Donald Currie's Castle Line, which commenced trading in 1862. Following the merger of the two companies in 1900 it owned and operated more than 100 vessels, but if the pre-merger ships are included the total comes to some 250.

Union-Castle, like other shipping lines, was always associated with a particular trade, in its case the routes to southern and eastern Africa. There was the express passenger and mail service to Cape Town and Durban from Southampton, inaugurated by the Union Line in 1863, and a slower round-Africa service from London to East African ports, either clockwise via the Mediterranean or anti-clockwise via the South Atlantic. Regular sailings were made in each service and the departures from Southampton, every Thursday at 4 o'clock, were legendary. The company also operated a fleet of fruit ships and cargo liners.

Unlike other shipping lines, Union-Castle did not turn to cruising when air travel eroded its core business in the 1970s. The only cruise ship it ever operated was the *Reina del Mar*, managed under charter to an economy travel organisation.

As a young shipping enthusiast living at Cowes in the early 1960s, I was able to see most of the lavender-hull, yacht-like Union-Castle liners as they sailed past the Isle of Wight, bound to and from Southampton. In those days, thanks to slower turn-rounds, there were usually at least two of these elegant ships berthed at Southampton's Western Docks, allowing a close-up view from the excursion craft that toured the port.

Union-Castle was a shipping line with a particularly good reputation as an employer and many local lads who went to sea chose careers aboard these popular ships, among them my good friends Francis Caldwell, William Thomas, Ron Saunders and Peter Clark, to name just a few, besides my brother-in-law Chris Morgan who served aboard the *Windsor Castle*, the company's largest ship.

Sadly, the Union-Castle ships are now long gone, no more than a fond recollection from down shipping's memory lane. The last of the ships to go, the former *Transvaal Castle*, ended her life as the cruise ship *Festivale*. Like all her predecessors, she looked incredibly modern and sleek to the very last. It had been that liner, under the name *S. A. Vaal*, which made the final sailing from Southampton on the Cape run on 12 September 1977, bringing the curtain down on a wonderful era.

Thanks go to Bill Miller for reviving the memory of those lovely Union-Castle ships in this book.

David L. Williams
Newport, Isle of Wight
January 2013

INTRODUCTION

While they were not especially familiar to me as I watched the great liners in my boyhood along the shores of the Hudson River, from Hoboken, New Jersey (just west of the great steamship piers of New York City), I certainly knew of the distant Union-Castle liners. They certainly appeared, often quite prominently, in the books by the great Laurence Dunn that I collected in those days – with titles such as *Liners and Their Recognition, Passenger Liners: Belfast Built* and, of course, the brilliant, encyclopedic twin volumes of *Passenger Liners*. There were also the small, softcover guide books such as *Ships of Southampton & the Solent*. In reading the statistics and realizing their comparative dimensions, many of the Union-Castle liners seemed to me to be very large. The *Pretoria Castle*, at 747 feet in length, was almost as large as, say, the *Nieuw Amsterdam* and longer than the likes of such celebrated New York liners as the *America, Caronia* and *Cristoforo Colombo*. The design of the big Union-Castle liners was also intriguing. They were long, low and carried comparatively few passengers when compared to their size. The Castle liners also had a noticeable rake, which hinted at their significant service speed.

In my boyhood in the 1950s, I often visited the great and grand Cunard Line offices in Manhattan, along Lower Broadway and which was dubbed 'Steamship Row'. Cunard itself and their vast liner fleet were the primary reasons for any visit, but off to one side in the main booking hall were displays of brochures, deck plans and sailing schedules from other British passenger ship companies. Union-Castle, then quite remote to me, had a sizeable presence as I recall. Each ship in the Castle fleet then had its own, thick, foldout deck plan and that not only included detailed plans but color photos of the ship and its interiors. I treasured these. Cunard offered a booking service, of course, wherein travelers could cross in as few as five days, say, on the *Queen Mary* or *Queen Elizabeth*, spend some time ashore and then connect to one of the Thursday afternoon sailings to the South African Cape on one of the big Mail Ships. Alternately, travelers could cross to London and be linked to one of the round-Africa departures.

In 1971, during a summer visit to London, a friend (who worked for an important New York City travel agent) and I visited Rotherwick House, which included Union-Castle's streetside booking office. I was especially dazzled by the huge builder's model of the *Windsor Castle*. We met one of the managers, who discovered our great fascination with ocean liners and, in great surprise, offered both of us a trip from Southampton to Madeira on the *Windsor Castle* and then a northbound return on the *S. A. Vaal*. Unfortunately, our summer plans were made – we had to decline. But what a missed opportunity.

While I never sailed on authentic Castle liners on their African voyages, I did make voyages on three of them in their subsequent lives – on the *Amerikanis*, the former *Kenya Castle*, on a sailing from New York to Bermuda in November 1969; onboard *The Victoria*, the ex-*Dunnottar Castle*, from San Juan to the so-called lower Caribbean in August 1988; and finally, in 1990, aboard the *Festivale*, the onetime *Transvaal Castle* and later *S. A. Vaal*, from Miami to the Eastern Caribbean. Otherwise, I recall seeing the *Windsor Castle* berthed at the Southampton docks on a misty July morning in 1973 from the decks of the inbound *France;* then the former *S. A. Vaal* being rebuilt at a Kobe shipyard in July 1978; and later the ex-*Pendennis Castle*, renamed as the *Sinbad I*, anchored in Hong Kong harbor from the decks of the 12-passenger containership *President Taft*

during that same summer of 1978. In April 1997, I gave a talk to the World Ship Society's Cape Town branch and the meeting room – bookcases, tables and especially chairs – included items offloaded from the likes of the *Edinburgh Castle* and *S. A. Oranje* (ex-*Pretoria Castle*) when they were en route to Far Eastern scrap yards in 1975–76.

Like Cunard, P&O and many other firms under the Red Ensign, Union-Castle was a very large, important and highly popular company. They are still remembered. On my current voyages, I often hear recollections and anecdotes from former passengers and crew as well as onlookers that watched from, say, the Southampton shorelines. Campbell McCutcheon of Amberley Publishing, who himself is a great ocean liner historian, writer and collector, suggested this title. I am delighted to follow through with this recollection of these Union-Castle liners in their final heyday. What a grand fleet – I can almost hear their whistles sounding for an afternoon sailing to the Cape!

Bill Miller
Secaucus, New Jersey
Winter 2013

EARLY CASTLE LINERS

Ocean liner nostalgia! We are docked (in April 2011 and aboard the luxury cruise ship *Crystal Serenity*) just across from Cape Town's old docks, the sheds (in seeming good, well-maintained order) and the vintage 1940s cranes (made in England and common to British and British-linked ports around the world) are still in place. The cranes are in fact lined in order, like good soldiers. It was at these docks that the bygone passenger ships once linked South Africa, mostly with Europe. There was until 1977 the great Union-Castle Line, British-flag of course, and which ran an express service that took thirteen days between Cape Town and Southampton – with a quick stop at either Madeira or Las Palmas en route. They had very famous ships, such as the *Windsor Castle*, *Pendennis Castle* and *Transvaal Castle*, and on which you could connect from New York on the likes of the old *Queen Mary* and *Queen Elizabeth*, each taking five days to cross the North Atlantic. Consequently, in a little over three weeks, one could travel from New York to South Africa via England. On the famed, class-divided Union-Castle Line, it was that great sense of pure transport for passengers as well as the mails and some freight of course (like tons and tons of gold bullion going up to the Bank of England in London). The first class passengers tended to be older and, of course, richer: top-draw businessmen, high government officials and aged aristocrats (who brought along their own servants, trunks of course and tended to sail in the southern winter and so escape the dread British winters). Down in lower-deck tourist class, you had students, bargain travelers and immigrants (lots of Brits in those days seeking new and supposedly better lives in South Africa). Tourists used to come and go for the famous garden tours as well as safaris. Union-Castle, one of the greatest of all shipping lines, was eventually done in by the jet (which stole their passengers) and by container ships (that grabbed their cargos). Today, Union-Castle is but memory and, now thirty-five years past, their waterfront offices at Southampton are converted to luxury apartments.

There were lots of other shipping lines to South Africa, of course. The Ellerman Lines had a quartet of yacht-like, 107-bed passenger ships on the London–South and East Africa run. Then there was the Holland-Africa Line out of Amsterdam and, from Italy, there was Lloyd Triestino's very smart *Africa* and *Europa*. New York-based Farrell Lines ran two passenger-cargo ships, the *African Endeavour* and *African Enterprise*, both of which carried up to eighty-two all-first class passengers, on the South African

Left: A splendid beginning of post-war Union-Castle liners: The four-funnel *Arundel Castle* sailing out of the Victoria Basin at Cape Town in a photo dated 1931. (Albert Wilhelmi Collection)

Right: When the *Arundel Castle* was scrapped in 1959, she was the last surviving ship to have been built with four funnels. (Albert Wilhelmi Collection)

run. Although retired in 1959, they were a businessmen's link – advertising seventeen days direct from Farrell's Brooklyn pier to the Cape Town docks. Up until the late 1960s, a long-haul service was on the Dutch-flag passenger ships of the Royal Interocean Lines, which made four-month voyages from Brazil and Argentina over to South Africa and then to Southeast Asia before heading up to Hong Kong and Japanese ports. These days, of course, it is all cruise ships that come to call at Cape Town.

Niche passenger ship travel! Berthed just across is the little, toy-like *St Helena*, a 3,000-tonner owned and operated by the British Government between Cape Town and two of the last outposts of the old Empire: the South Atlantic islands of Ascension and, expectedly, St Helena itself. The 22-year old ship is the vital link – 128 passengers, cargo, supplies and of course the mail. She is in fact the very last legitimate 'Royal Mail Ship'. Built up in Scotland, she is quite adorable – a blue-colored hull, superstructure placed aft and a buff-colored single funnel. Containers are crammed, it seems, along the very limited, open fore decks. True passenger ship travelers have or want to travel on the charmingly unique, almost eccentric *St Helena*. She's unique in a passenger ship world of huge, all-white, multi-deck cruise ships. Interestingly, the 6,400-passenger *Allure of the Sea*, which we sailed aboard three months before, in January 2011, is seventy times larger than the little *St Helena*.

Union-Castle had a long, rich and colorful – and important – history. It could trace its roots, its varied and rich heritage, to two companies. Founded in 1853, the Union Line started as the Southampton Shipping Company, created to transport coal from South Wales to the port of Southampton. It was soon renamed the Union Steam Collier Company, then the Union Steamship Company and finally, in 1857, the Union Line. That same year it was awarded a lucrative contract: to carry mail between Southampton and South Africa, then referred to as the Cape Colony.

At about the same time, Donald Currie created the Castle Packet Company for a service from England out to India, to Calcutta, but via the South African Cape. This service was substantially curtailed, however, after the opening of the Suez Canal in 1869 and so Currie's renamed Castle Line, and later the Castle Mail Packet Company, began running instead to South Africa.

In 1872, with the reorganization of the Cape Colony, mail services to and from Britain were more firmly set and shipping contracts re-negotiated. Four years later, and to avoid any monopolies, the prized mail contract was awarded jointly to two companies – the Union Line and the Castle Mail Packet Company. The contract included specifications for safe, reliable but speedy delivery of the mails. This joint contract expired finally, but then led to greater cooperation between the two ship owners and best seen for the transport of troops and equipment during the Boer War. Merger seemed the likely option and so, on 8 March 1900, the two firms joined together to form the Union-Castle Mail Steamship Company Limited. Service was established with strict timetables aboard ships bearing Castle Mail Packet Line names, painted with lavender hulls and capped by red-painted funnels with black tops. It was agreed that every Thursday afternoon at 4 o'clock a Union-Castle Mail Ship would depart from Southampton and that at the same time a ship would sail from Cape Town.

Union-Castle was bought by the Royal Mail Lines in 1911, but continued to maintain its separate identity. But when Royal Mail and its parent ran into great financial difficulties in 1932, at the height of the worldwide Depression, Union-Castle Line again became an independent company. The company was merged into British & Commonwealth Shipping in 1956, but then withdrew from shipping altogether in 1982 and itself was liquidated completely in 1990. Briefly, the Union-Castle name was specially revived in 1999 for a centenary commemorative cruise aboard the liner *Victoria*, chartered from P&O.

Expectedly, Union-Castle served heroically during the two world wars. And expectedly, there were considerable losses. In the Second World War, the company lost thirteen ships – out of thirty-one in the fleet when the War started in September 1939.

Above left: A view dated 1924, for the opening of the floating dry dock, of the flag-dressed *Arundel Castle* in the large floating dock at Southampton. (J&C McCutcheon Collection)

Above right: A wonderful post card view of the four-funnel *Arundel Castle*. (J&C McCutcheon Collection)

Left: After being rebuilt in 1937, the *Arundel Castle* became, according to many onlookers, a better-looking ship with two funnels and a raked bow. (Albert Wilhelmi Collection)

The splendid *Arundel Castle* at sea. (David Williams Collection).

A fine but sentimental color view dated 5 December 1958. Dressed in flags, the *Arundel Castle* is heading off on her final northbound voyage to the UK. (Albert Wilhelmi Collection)

LLANSTEPHAN CASTLE

'At last came the summer of 1945 and the world breathed a sigh of relief. Men of armies in every corner of the globe laid down their arms, celebrated the coming of peace and then turned their thoughts to the promised bright new world.' So wrote authors W. H. Mitchell & L. A. Sawyer in *The Cape Run*, their splendid history of Union-Castle Line. After considerable war losses, Union-Castle was left with six big Cape Mail passenger ships, six Round Africa passenger ships, five refrigerated cargo ships and two general cargo ships. Symbolically, just before the War ended, on 2 April 1945, a ten-year Ocean Mail & Ocean Freight Contract was signed and the provisions for renewal – including construction of two 28,000-grt mail ships, the largest yet for Union-Castle.

The eldest post-war survivor was the 520-ft long *Llanstephan Castle*, which had been built by Fairfield Shipbuilding & Engineering Company at Glasgow and commissioned in the spring of 1914, just before the First World War broke out. After serving as a troopship in that war, she served on the Cape Mail run, the East African service and the new Round Africa run, which had first begun in 1922. A coal-burner, she was not converted to oil fuel until as late as 1938. She was again used as a trooper in the Second World War, lastly serving with the Royal Indian Navy and being

assigned to the East Indies. She was reconditioned in 1946–47, to carry as few as 420 passengers – 220 in first class and 200 in tourist class. By then, of course, she was merely a fill-in, awaiting new, post-war tonnage.

John Dimmock, who later became one of Union-Castle's best known chief pursers, was posted in the *Llanstephan Castle* in the ship's final years. 'The little *Llanstephan Castle* – she was only just over 11,000 tons – sailed out of London on our Round Africa service,' he recalled. 'She did the "out west" direction – calling at Las Palmas, Ascension, St Helena, Cape Town, Port Elizabeth, East London, Durban, Lourenco Marques, Beira, Dar-es-Salaam, Zanzibar, Tanga, Mombasa, Aden, Port Sudan, Suez, Port Said, Genoa, Marseilles and Gibraltar. I especially remember that the best cabin onboard the *Llanstephan Castle* – with private toilet and bath – cost 100 pounds in 1950 for the 3½ week voyage to Cape Town. In those years, we carried lots and lots of British civil servants, "crown agents people" as they were also called, and mostly out to what was then colonial East Africa. There wasn't any air conditioning in such elderly ships and instead we relied on the old Punkah forced air ventilation system. Fortunately, and particularly in the first class section, there were lots of outside cabins or rooms that had at least some form of open-air exposure. In the holds, we carried general cargo southbound and then brought large amounts of copper and coffee on the homeward runs. In those sweltering African ports, we had to use good sense and allow the crew to work at their own pace. It seemed that most tasks were done over longer periods. When we returned after those 3-month-long round trips, we had three weeks in the London Docks. That period was considered shore leave and then you returned in time for the next sailing.'

At the age of thirty-eight, the 14-knot *Llanstephan Castle* was decommissioned in February 1952 and then scrapped at Newport in Wales.

Above: This view from 1949 shows the *Arundel Castle* berthed along Southampton's New Docks with the *Aquitania* and *Queen Elizabeth* beyond, and the *Queen Mary* on the far right. (J&C McCutcheon Collection)

Right: South into the Sun: A superb post-war poster depicting the *Arundel Castle*. (Albert Wilhelmi Collection)

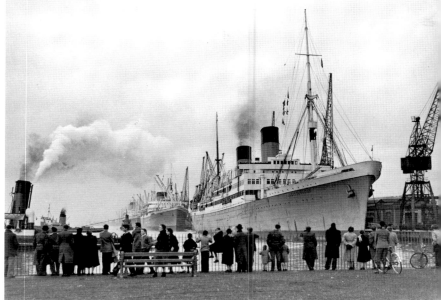

Left: A spectacular view from late 1958 of Southampton's New Docks – the soon-to-be-scrapped *Arundel Castle* is at the right; then the brand new *Pendennis Castle*, *Pretoria Castle*, *Queen Mary* and, in the King George V Graving Dock, the *Queen Elizabeth*. (J&C McCutcheon Collection)

Right: Bound for Hong Kong and the breakers: Onlookers watch as the *Arundel Castle* departs on her final voyage. (Author's Collection)

Right: In her original guise with two squat funnels and blunt bow, the *Carnarvon Castle* is seen at Cape Town in a view from 28 March 1933. (Albert Wilhelmi Collection)

Left: A very basic, almost no-nonsense ship: the *Llandovery Castle.* (Union-Castle Line).

ARUNDEL CASTLE

Purser John Dimmock was posted to the *Arundel Castle* in the late 1940s. 'This grand old ship was retained by the British Government for some years after the war, until as late as the fall of 1949. We sailed mostly to Port Said via Gibraltar and Malta. Mostly, we carried Royal Air Force and Royal Navy personnel. The original first class was used by the military officers, who had metal beds. Otherwise, the old second and third class sections had been made into huge dormitories for the troops.'

The *Arundel Castle* was actually a First World War liner, having been laid down at Belfast in 1915 as the *Amroth Castle*. Work soon ceased and she laid on the stocks for four years when, as the renamed *Arundel Castle*, she was launched in September 1919 and then commissioned in April 1921. She and her sister, the *Windsor Castle* (sunk while in war service off North Africa in March 1943), were the largest Union-Castle liners yet and the only liners with four funnels (the fourth being a dummy) apart from those on the North Atlantic. These sister ships were the sensations of the day and consequently very popular. First class was especially luxurious and, of course, an improvement over prior Castle liners. It was noted, 'First class cabins are all large and are all porthole staterooms. They have wardrobes, chests of drawers, folding wash basins, mirrors and reading lights over all beds. The beds are all of the "cot" type – of white enamel, fitted with sanitary spring mattresses and, in certain cabins, with Pullman beds. Private Suites consist of sitting room, bedroom, bathroom and maid's room. There are easy chairs, a writing desk and a bookcase cabinet. The floors are covered in parquet linoleum, overlaid with rugs. Provision is made for heating, created by vapor radiators that can be operated at will by passengers.'

In a fleetwide modernization program in the latter half of the 1930s, the *Arundel Castle* (and her sister) underwent a long reconditioning during 1937. The four funnels came off, replaced by two of more modern styling. In the process, these two ships became much more attractive looking.

The *Arundel Castle* was the last of the company's ships to be reconditioned following war. She had extended post-war duties as a troopship. She finally returned to the Express run in October 1950 – with her accommodations then upgraded and refitted for 164 in first class and 371 in tourist class. At the time, the weekly sailing sequence of sailing from Southampton was: *Pretoria Castle, Arundel Castle, Athlone Castle, Carnarvon Castle, Edinburgh Castle, Winchester Castle, Capetown Castle* and *Stirling Castle*.

The *Arundel Castle* seemed to go on for ever and ever – and remained popular to the very end. In April 1957, she reached a Union-Castle milestone – she had completed 200 voyages on the South African run. 'She was the grandmother of the fleet in her last years,' added John Dimmock. 'She was a fine looking, popular ship to the very end.'

When she was finally retired in December 1958, the *Arundel Castle* was the last surviving liner to have been built with four funnels. She had sailed for nearly thirty-eight years, steaming some 3.5 million miles in all. She was sold to Hong Kong breakers, but actually was to have been leased first to a Hollywood director for use as the fictional trans-Pacific liner *Claridon,* which explodes and partially sinks in the drama *The Last Voyage.* Schedules did not quite match properly, however, and the part went instead to the far larger *Ile de France,* which had just been sold to Japanese scrappers. The 19,216-grt *Arundel Castle* then ranked as the largest ship to be scrapped at Hong Kong. Her furniture, fittings and even artwork were auctioned off just before the dismantling began. The shipbreaking firm also owned a clock-making factory and it was often said that some of the remains of the *Arundel Castle* found their way into alarm clocks!

Above: Wartime: The *Carnarvon Castle* is seen here as a high-capacity trooper in 1944. (Cronican-Arroyo Collection)

Below: Post-war: Not yet fully restored and refitted, the *Carnarvon Castle* is shown here in 1948 while being used in low-fare migrant service to South Africa. (Alex Duncan)

LLANDOVERY CASTLE

The London-Round Africa service was all but depleted by the end of the Second World War, in 1945–46. Simply, there were too few ships – there had been war losses, other ships retained for further Government service and still others being reassigned to the more pressing, more important Cape Mail Express. It was the 10,639-grt *Llandovery Castle* – with post-war accommodations for 215 first class and 198 tourist class passengers, and considerable cargo space – which reopened the Round Africa service with a sailing from London in May 1947. The similar-sized *Llangibby Castle* and then the *Llanstephan Castle* soon followed in this service.

In 1950, the sailing sequence from London for the Round Africa service was: *Durban Castle, Dunnottar Castle, Llanstephen Castle, Warwick Castle, Llandovery Castle* and *Llangibby Castle.*

Completed in September 1925, the 487-ft long *Llandovery Castle* was the first new, post-First World War liner for the Round Africa service. During the Second World War, however, and when she served as a hospital ship, she seemed almost a magnet to enemy attacks. She was bombed during the Blitz over Southampton in November 1940, then again at Suez in November 1941 and then three times in the Mediterranean in 1942–43. Always repaired, she endured – by the end of the war, in 1945, she had transported 38,000 sick and wounded. She was broken-up in 1953.

Above left: Mini mail ship: The *Llangibby Castle* was a shorter version of the big mail ships, but another squat funneled-design in vogue in the 1920s. (Union-Castle Line)

Above right: End of the line: The *Llangibby Castle* leaving London and going off to the breakers in the summer of 1954. (Union-Castle Line)

Below: The smart-looking *Winchester Castle* after being rebuilt and modernized in 1938 with a large single funnel. (Cronican-Arroyo Collection)

Left: The *Winchester Castle* seen berthed at Port Elizabeth in a photo dated 24 March 1958. (Albert Wilhelmi Collection)

Right: Another view of the *Winchester Castle*, but seen here departing from Durban. (Albert Wilhelmi Collection)

619 Castle Liner leaving Durban

The *Carnarvon Castle* at Southampton on 21 July 1958. (Kenneth Wightman, courtesy of Mick Lindsay)

CARNARVON CASTLE

From the very end of the Second World War, many in Britain looked to better, more prosperous lives (and perhaps even better weather conditions) elsewhere. Australia would become the primary destination – and this would last well into the 1970s. The huge island nation was seen by many as a 'palm tree-lined paradise – with an open class system and limitless opportunity.' South Africa had prospered, even during the war years, and this was highlighted by the discovery of gold in the Orange Free State in the spring of 1946. Soon afterward, there was supposedly great opportunity in the groundnut scheme in southern Tanganyika and this was followed by the general expansion in both Northern and Southern Rhodesia. The imaginations of many war-weary, sometimes jobless, post-war, potential migrants was aroused. They soon looked to book passage – a new life in South Africa beckoned.

The South African Government was interested and created attractive passage schemes. The Government approached Union-Castle – could the company provide ships with quarters suited to these migrants? Quickly, the London headquarters reacted: the post-war reconditioning of at least three liners would be postponed and instead these ex-troopships would be given only minimal refits and then began sailing as comparatively austere, one-class ships. The *Carnarvon Castle* made the first such sailing, in June 1947, and was booked to capacity when she departed from the Southampton Docks – 1,283 passengers in all. The *Winchester Castle* followed, with a one-class capacity listed as 877, and then the *Arundel Castle*, carrying 846. This service lasted for almost two years, until May 1949. Altogether, this trio of Union-Castle migrant ships had transported 30,000 British migrants to South and East Africa.

The 20,141-grt *Carnarvon Castle* was then restored properly and returned to the Cape Mail Express (carrying up to 617 passengers in two classes). She had been completed back in the summer of 1926, but as a squat-topped, twin-funneled ship. She became more far more attractive during a full modernization and refit in 1937 – now, she had a single, large, flat funnel, which became something of the Union-Castle style – and was lengthened by thirty feet and receiving a raked bow. She had a valiant war career, which included an encounter with a Nazi raider, the *Thor*, in the South Atlantic.

In 1960, as the *Carnarvon Castle* was nearing the end of her days, Union-Castle was perhaps at its final zenith. Altogether, the company had no less than fourteen liners. On the Cape Mail Service, the Line used its largest and finest liners: *Carnarvon Castle, Winchester Castle,* the sisters *Athlone Castle* and *Stirling Castle, Capetown Castle,* another set of sisters

– the *Edinburgh Castle* and *Pretoria Castle*, the new *Pendennis Castle* (commissioned in 1959) and finally the *Windsor Castle* (which set off on her maiden voyage in August 1960). Still to come was the *Transvaal Castle*, which would be, in fact, the very last passenger ship to be built for the company even if further new tonnage was being considered. The Cape Mail Service still seemed a very viable and profitable operation.

'We would leave Southampton on a Thursday afternoon, make a quick stop at Las Palmas or Madeira and be in Cape Town two weeks later, also on a Thursday,' according to John Havers, former purser on many post-war Castle liners. 'On Friday, we'd sail from Cape Town and then there would be Port Elizabeth on Sunday, East London on Monday and finally Durban on Tuesday. In the Atlantic and elsewhere, our ships used to pass one another at sea, often at a combined 30–35 knots, and this gave the passengers what we called the '30 second thrill'.'

'In first class, we had the equivalent of first and club classes on today's airliners,' added Havers. 'We'd have the high professionals, the bankers, industrialists, corporate chairmen, aristocracy and the older, well-heeled "winter dodgers". Princess Alice, Harold Macmillan and many South African Government officials were among our passengers. Union-Castle to the Cape was very popular. But actually, another British passenger ship company, the Ellerman Lines, was considered to be the finest on the South African run while the Holland-Africa Line was second. Union-Castle was actually rated as third.'

The *Carnarvon Castle* sailed for thirty-six years, being replaced in the summer of 1962 by the new *Transvaal Castle*. The older ship soon went off, with a reduced crew, to the breakers at Mihara in Japan.

Above: The *Winchester Castle* departing from Southampton. (Roger Sherlock)

Below: 1930s sleek and smart: The handsome 725-ft long *Athlone Castle* seen on her sea trials in the spring of 1936. (Cronican-Arroyo Collection)

Above left: A sunny summer's afternoon: The *Athlone Castle* departing from Cape Town. (Albert Wilhelmi Collection)

Above right: A first class double aboard the *Athlone Castle* (Norman Knebel Collection)

Below left: A first class single room onboard the *Stirling Castle* (Norman Knebel Collection)

Opposite
Above left: The *Athlone Castle* at the Duncan Dock in Cape Town in a photo dated January 12, 1956. (Albert Wilhelmi Collection)

Above right: The cover of a passenger list dated 7 March 1963 from the *Athlone Castle* (but showing the *Pendennis Castle* on the cover). (J&C McCutcheon Collection)

Below left: A splendid stern view of the *Athlone Castle*, with the *Windsor Castle* just beyond. (J&C McCutcheon Collection)

UNION-CASTLE

LIST OF PASSENGERS

330

R.M.M.V. " ATHLONE CASTLE "

From Southampton · 7th March, 1963.

LLANGIBBY CASTLE

Harry Andrews, a chemical engineer, and his wife Julia were residents of East Africa for over thirty years. They were also great enthusiasts of passenger ships and sea travel. Their records are most impressive, having sailed in almost 200 different ships. According to Mr Andrews, 'We have always avoided, or tried to avoid, air travel. We have always kept abreast of the international shipping schedules and have even noted those unusual, sometimes once-a-year voyages. My father was a civil servant in colonial East Africa and so we travelled, beginning in the 1930s, but excepting the war years, at least every two years, but sometimes once a year, to and from Britain. We sailed in almost all of the Union-Castle Line passenger ships, beginning with the *Llangibby Castle*. Often, we sailed from Durban and by way of East London, Port Elizabeth and Capetown and then onward to Southampton or London via Las Palmas or Madeira. I especially recall liners like the *Arundel Castle*, *Capetown Castle*, *Athlone Castle* and *Pretoria Castle*. Altogether, I had some forty years of travel with Union-Castle. Many years later, in August 1977, it somehow seemed rather fitting that we should be onboard the final Union-Castle sailing in the *Windsor Castle*.'

Built by Harland & Wolff at their Glasgow yard in 1929, the 11,951-grt, 507-ft long *Llangibby Castle* was rather eccentric in exterior design – two twin squat funnels were placed close together and far forward, and altogether gave her a stubby, cut-short look. Used on the Round Africa service, she had a very adventurous wartime career – she was torpedoed, when outbound from the UK for Singapore with troops, in January 1942. Her stern was blown off and, wallowing in a fierce gale, she managed to reach the Azores at a much reduced speed of 9 knots and being steered in very erratic fashion by her propellers. Later, she managed to reach Gibraltar, had temporary repairs (lasting fifty-seven days) and then, again very slowly, made her way back to the UK for full repairs. She was very useful thereafter – making the likes of seventy trips with invasion forces across the English Channel as part of the Normandy landings.

She finished her days at a scrap yard in Wales in the summer of 1954.

Above left: The *Stirling Castle* in Durban Bay. (Albert Wilhelmi Collection)

Above right: The *Stirling Castle* and her sister were among the most handsome of the big Union-Castle mail ships. (Albert Wilhelmi Collection)

Below right: Late afternoon at East London: The *Stirling Castle* departs on another line voyage. (Albert Wilhelmi Collection)

Above left: The *Athlone Castle* at Southampton's New Docks. (Kenneth Wightman Collection, courtesy of David Williams)

Below left: With the dramatic background of Table Mountain, the *Stirling Castle* makes another departure. (Robert Pabst Collection)

Below right: Another beautiful mail liner: The *Capetown Castle* heads off. (Albert Wilhelmi Collection)

Above left: A fine artist's rendering of the *Capetown Castle*. (Albert Wilhelmi Collection)

Above right: The *Capetown Castle* leaving the King George V Graving Dock at Southampton. (Kenneth Wightman Collection, courtesy of David Williams)

WINCHESTER CASTLE

'I was born just before World War II started, in Rhodesia in East Africa, and went to sea at nineteen, sailing on British passenger ships. I started with the Union-Castle Line and began sailing on one of their oldest ships of the time [the late '50s], the *Winchester Castle* and then went over to the *Durban Castle* and *Edinburgh Castle*,' recalled Harry Gunston. 'They were grand old ships in many ways, very well run, popular with British passengers and were in many ways like "floating England" – they were part of the great British connection out in Africa. They were also exceptionally punctual. We always seemed to arrive and sail on time!'

The 20,001-grt *Winchester Castle*, built at Belfast and delivered in late 1930, had a classic motor ship look of that period – a long, low superstructure topped off by two squat funnels. She and her twin sister, the *Warwick Castle* (lost in the Second World War), were modernized in 1938 and given the typical Union-Castle single funnel: raked, flat, low and centered. Used as a hardworking trooper during the war years, she was restored in 1948 – for 186 first class and 400 tourist class passengers – and sailed until broken-up in Japan in 1960.

Opposite:
Above left: The *Capetown Castle* docked at Durban. (Albert Wilhelmi Collection)

Above right: A passenger list from the *Carnarvon Castle*, dated 25 June 1937. (J&C McCutcheon Collection)

Below left: A fine bow view of the very popular *Capetown Castle*. (J&C McCutcheon Collection)

UNION-CASTLE LINE

THE DRAKENSBERG MOUNTAINS, NATAL.

LIST OF PASSENGERS

R.M.M.V. "Carnarvon Castle"
leaving Southampton 25th June, 1937.

Left: The *Capetown Castle* sailing from Table Bay for coastal ports on 23 June 1955. (Albert Wilhelmi Collection)

Right: The *Dunnottar Castle* had a long career that lasted sixty-two years. (Roger Sherlock).

UNION-CASTLE LINE TO SOUTH and EAST AFRICA

Left: An artist's rendering of the *Durban Castle*. (Albert Wilhelmi Collection)

Right: The former *Dunnottar Castle,* but as the vastly rebuilt Chandris cruise ship *The Victoria*, photographed at Martinique in 1988. (Author's Collection)

Left: An aerial view of the *Warwick Castle*. (Union-Castle Line)

Below left: The *Durban Castle* had just arrived at the scrappers in Hamburg in the spring of 1962. (Steffen Weirauch Collection)

Below right: Unrecognizable, the pre-war *Pretoria Castle* was greatly rebuilt and used as an aircraft carrier during World War II. (J&C McCutcheon Collection)

STIRLING CASTLE

Harry Andrews and his wife all but 'commuted' between Britain and South and East Africa in the 1950s and '60s. 'The big Union-Castle mail ships were splendid ships – I well remember trips in the *Stirling Castle*, *Capetown Castle* and, those post-war "sensations", the *Edinburgh Castle* and *Pretoria Castle*. They were superbly served and fed, but with a conservative, almost quiet atmosphere that was typical of British passenger ships in those days. It often seemed that these ships were like great, big, floating clubs – everyone appeared to know everyone else: the officers, the stewards and the waiters, and of course the passengers.'

The 725-ft long *Stirling Castle* and her twin sister, the *Athlone Castle*, were among the finest looking liners of their day – they were long, low, sleek, powerful-looking. Their single funnels all but dominated their appearances, being 32 feet wide and as much as 50 feet in height. First introduced in February 1936, the 25,554-grt, 20-knot *Stirling Castle* actually set a record that summer – Southampton to the Cape in 13 days and 9 hours.

Carrying up to 243 first class and 540 tourist class passengers after wartime service as a troopship, the *Stirling Castle* was finally retired at the end of 1965. Early in the next year, she was delivered to Japanese scrappers at Mihara.

Left: The *Durban Castle* being demolished in the summer of 1962. (Steffen Weirauch Collection)

Right: Classic Union-Castle refrigerated cargo vessel – the 8,300grt *Rustenburg Castle* seen at Cape Town in 1971. (Albert Wilhelmi Collection)

Above: Post-war sensation: The mighty *Edinburgh Castle* arriving at Cape Town. (Albert Wilhelmi Collection)

Right: An exciting Union-Castle Line poster featuring the *Edinburgh Castle* and dating from 1953. (Albert Wilhelmi Collection)

Above: The *Pretoria Castle* in a scene dated October 1956. (Albert Wilhelmi Collection)

Left: Dating from the late 1950s, the cover of a foldout deck plan for the *Pretoria Castle*. (Andrew Kilk Collection).

ATHLONE CASTLE

After also having been a wartime troopship, the *Athlone Castle* had a year of reconditioning to full passenger status in 1946–47. She was the third mail ship to return after the war, rejoining the run to the Cape in April 1947. Her sister, the *Stirling Castle*, was soon to follow. At that time, Union-Castle hoped to have another mail ship restored and back in service every three months. The goal was full resumption by 1948, and it being crowned by the arrivals of the biggest mail liners yet, the *Pretoria Castle* and *Edinburgh Castle*. There were new, almost pressing demands that came about – the need for low-fare migrant ships to South and East Africa. Consequently, three mail ships – the *Carnarvon Castle, Winchester Castle* and *Arundel Castle* – were not restored according to the planned schedule, but pressed into temporary service as low-fare, one-class migrant ships. Full resumption of the Cape Mail Express was delayed.

Launched at Belfast in November 1935, the *Athlone Castle* was appropriately named by Princess Alice, Countess of Athlone who was one of her Union-Castle long-standing passengers. Princess Alice often tried to travel on a sailing of the *Athlone Castle,* which she called 'her ship'. Decommissioned in the summer of 1965, the 780-passenger *Athlone Castle* was sent out to Kaohsiung on Taiwan and demolished.

Left: A dramatic view of the departing *Pretoria Castle*. (Gillespie-Faber Collection)

Right: Another very fine view of the *Pretoria Castle*. (Albert Wilhelmi Collection)

Above: A broadside of the *Pretoria Castle.* (Alex Duncan)

Right: The Southampton Docks: A view from the *Braemar Castle* looking to the *Pretoria Castle.* It is dated June 1955. (Roger Sherlock)

Left: The *Pretoria Castle* berthed at Southampton. (Union-Castle Line)

Below left: The smartly decorated Long Gallery aboard the *Edinburgh Castle.* (Union-Castle Line)

Below right: The *Edinburgh Castle* departing from Cape Town. (Albert Wilhelmi Collection)

DUNNOTTAR CASTLE

I last saw the former *Dunnottar Castle* at Lisbon, berthed in the inner harbor, during the summer of 1998. Together with two other passenger ships, the *World Explorer* (a vessel with a long list of former names – *La Guardia*, *Leilani*, *President Roosevelt*, *Atlantis* and *Emerald Seas*) and the *Italia Prima* (the rebuilt former *Stockholm* of *Andrea Doria* collision and sinking fame), the three ships were serving as moored hotels for the city's extravagant Expo. In fact, there were few guests onboard and, after boarding for a walk-around, the veteran ship seemed to be ours. It was quite nostalgic. I well remembered her from her second life, from her New York-based sailing days as the *Victoria*. Then she belonged to the very popular Incres Line. I later sailed in her, in August 1989, during her third life as the Greek-owned, slightly renamed *The Victoria*. By that last visit at Lisbon, she was then one of the oldest liners still about. 'She is still a modern lady on the outside, but a grandmother, a great-grandmother, in other ways, behind the scenes, on the inside,' said her Egyptian first officer. She was, in fact, finally finished-off a few years later, in the summer of 2004 along the ship-breaking beaches of Alang in India.

She had a long history. Built by Harland & Wolff at Belfast in Northern Ireland, she was commissioned in June 1936 as the *Dunnottar Castle*. She then carried passengers (260 in first class, 240 in tourist) as well as lots of cargo on the Union-Castle Line's Round Africa service. She made those nine-week voyages that completely circled the African continent. Used during the Second World War as an armed merchant cruiser and then as a troopship, from 1939 until 1947, she resumed Union-Castle service until she was retired and put up for sale in 1958.

The Incres Line bought her to become their new, high-standard flagship, joining the veteran *Nassau* in New York cruise service. Sent to Holland, she was gutted down to the hull, re-engined as well (new Fiat diesels went aboard) and she was transformed into a modern, all-first class cruise liner. All-white and capped by a sleek yellow and blue funnel with a mast attached, she was renamed *Victoria* (even if Italy's Lloyd Triestino was operating a passenger ship with the same name at the same time). She had very modern Mediterranean decor for her 600 passengers, each of them now in cabins with a private bathroom. Her other amenities included complete air-conditioning, a twin-pool Lido Deck, a bi-level theatre, alternate buffet restaurant and several large suites. Generally, she made ten–eighteen day cruises from New York, almost always to the sunny Caribbean. On occasion, especially in summer, she made longer, more expensive trips to Northern Europe, Scandinavia and the Mediterranean.

By then a single-ship operator, Incres collapsed into bankruptcy during the great fuel oil price increases of 1975. The *Victoria* was laid-up and all but abandoned in New York harbor, at the unused Brooklyn Army Terminal. Her story continued, however. Chandris Cruises revived her two years later as *The Victoria* and used her mostly in the Caribbean out of San Juan, but also in summertime from Amsterdam to Scandinavia and the Baltic, and on occasion from Genoa to Mediterranean ports. Her last owner, beginning in 1992, was the Cypriot-based Louis Cruise Lines, who sailed her on short, two and three night Eastern Mediterranean itineraries but as the *Princesa Victoria*. After the charter at Lisbon, in 1998, the 62-year-old ship was laid-up and left to rust near Piraeus in Greece. Before going to the scrappers, there was a misplaced rumor (in 1999) that she was to go to Saudi Arabia to become a floating hotel.

Above: Daybreak: The *Edinburgh Castle* arriving at the Table Bay docks on 31 January 1963. (Albert Wilhelmi Collection)

Below: The *Edinburgh Castle* berthed along the New Docks with P&O's *Himalaya* in the distance. (J&C McCutcheon Collection)

Above left: Three Castle ships seen moored together during the Seamen's Strike in a view dated 20 July 1966 – the *Good Hope Castle, Southampton Castle* and *S. A. Oranje.* (J&C McCutcheon Collection)

Above right: Artist J. K. Byass's rendition of the *Edinburgh Castle.* (Albert Wilhelmi Collection)

Right: The Smoking Room aboard the *Edinburgh Castle.* (Norman Knebel Collection)

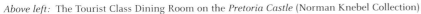

Above left: The Tourist Class Dining Room on the *Pretoria Castle* (Norman Knebel Collection)

Above right: Library and Writing Room on the *S. A. Oranje.* (Norman Knebel Collection)

Below right: A four-berth Tourist Class cabin aboard the *Pretoria Castle.* (Norman Knebel Collection)

Opposite:
Above left: Edinburgh Castle: The Long Gallery in First Class. (Norman Knebel Collection)

Above right: Edinburgh Castle: The attractive First Class Dining Room. (Norman Knebel Collection)

Below left: A first class single aboard the *Pretoria Castle.* (Norman Knebel Collection)

Below right: The sitting room of a suite aboard the *Pretoria Castle.* (Norman Knebel Collection)

CAPETOWN CASTLE

After use as a Second World War trooper, the 27,002-grt *Capetown Castle* – the company's flagship – was reconditioned quickly, in 1946, for restoration of peacetime services. Appropriately, she was the first liner to sail on the Mail Service following the war, departing from Southampton on 9 January 1947. All of her pre-war passenger fittings, including artworks, were taken out of storage and returned to the ship. She was now, however, better suited to post-war standards – with more spacious berthing of 250 in first class and 550 in tourist class. For a time, in 1947–48, and as other company liners continued in post-war trooping and austerity passenger service, the 734-ft long *Capetown Castle* was assisted, in weekly sailings from Southampton, by far smaller refrigerated cargo ships, none of which, however, carried passengers.

The *Capetown Castle* ranked as the longest motorliner afloat after she was first introduced in April 1938. She was also the first Castle liner to bear a name other than a British castle or fortress. Used as a heroic trooper during the war years, she made headlines twice in the 1960s. On 17 October 1960, she suffered an engine room explosion while sailing off Las Palmas. Sadly, seven crew members were killed. Then, on a northbound sailing in early 1965, there was further headlines: twenty gold ingots (worth £100,000) were stolen from the ship's strong room. The stash was actually not uncovered until her next sailing – it had been cemented into the bottoms of the sand lockers between the cargo holds on the lower decks.

The *Capetown Castle* had a long life. She was too slow for the accelerated mail service inaugurated in 1965, however she was kept on to run a budget 'extra service' – from Southampton and occasionally via Flushing in Holland to the Cape. This lasted for two years. In September 1967, after 180 voyages to South Africa on her record, she was handed over to Italian demolition crews at La Spezia.

Right: The cover of a foldout deck plan for the *Edinburgh Castle* dated 1967. (Andrew Kilk Collection)

Far right: Another deck plan cover, this one dated 1970. (Andrew Kilk Collection)

Left: The *S. A. Oranje* seen in her final days, in a photo dated July 1975. (Albert Wilhelmi Collection)

Right: Another sailing day for the *S. A. Oranje.* (Albert Wilhelmi Collection)

DURBAN CASTLE

As a young assistant purser, John Havers served on Union-Castle's East African service. There were six liners assigned to that service by the mid-1950s, sailing from London and occasionally making an outbound call at Rotterdam. 'There was the trio of sisters, the *Braemar Castle*, *Kenya Castle* and *Rhodesia Castle*; and three ships from the late 1930s, the *Dunnottar Castle*, *Durban Castle* and *Warwick Castle*', recalled Havers. 'Actually, a seventh Castle liner assisted somewhat, the 1950-built *Bloemfontein Castle*. The '50s were still boom years for such ships, which carried passengers as well as lots of cargo.'

Built in 1938 at Belfast, the *Durban Castle* was reconditioned after extensive wartime duties as a troopship and then as a landing ship, and resumed commercial sailing in June 1947. But due to pressing demands, she did not go back on the Round Africa service at first, but substituted on the faster, more important express run to the Cape. Later, she returned to her Round Africa itineraries, where she would spend the rest of her days.

By 1960, this Round Africa service was reduced slightly to five ships – the sisters *Durban Castle* and *Warwick Castle*, and the newer trio of *Braemar Castle*, *Kenya Castle* and *Rhodesia Castle*. John Havers noted, 'These ships sailed from the London Docks and alternated their itineraries: one voyage out by the Mediterranean, Suez and East African ports before returning to London via the Atlantic and the next trip out by the Atlantic side, then rounding the Cape and homeward via the East Coast, Suez and the Mediterranean. When these ships called at Genoa, passengers could connect by train to and from London and thereby saving five-seven sea days and avoiding the often notorious Bay of Biscay.'

'On the old Round & East Africa service, we'd have British civil servants, the tea and coffee planters, the copper workers, the mine managers, civilian troops, the missionaries and priests, the local inter-port passengers and the occasional special guest such as His Excellency the Governor General of the Sudan,' remembered Havers. 'Onboard entertainment was arranged by the purser's office in those days. There were cricket matches and games on deck, horse-racing, the Crossing-of-the-Line ceremony, dancing (some ships used records), indoor games, cards, fancy dress (held separately for adults and for children), the ship's concert (actually a passenger talent show) and then a separate prize night. As a purser, I earned $1,200 a month in the early 1960s.'

Purser John Dimmock was assigned to the *Durban Castle* in the late 1940s and in the '50s. 'When I was first assigned to the *Durban Castle*

Left: A trio of grand liners at Southampton in the 1960s – the *S. A. Oranje, Iberia* and *Canberra*. (J&C McCutcheon Collection)

Right: A great gathering of idle liners during the decisive Maritime Strike in May 1966. The *Franconia* and *Southern Cross* are in the upper left; then the *S. A. Oranje* and *Capetown Castle*. The *Queen Mary* is in the center. The *Caronia* and *Pendennis Castle* are in the top right. The *Franconia* and *Andes* are in the lower center. (Southern Newspapers Ltd)

Above left: The 18,400-grt, all one-class *Bloemfontein Castle* of 1950 was Union-Castle's 'odd duckling'. (Union-Castle Line)

Above right: The *Bloemfontein Castle* but in her later life as Chandris Lines' *Patris*. The view dates from 8 January 1973. (V. H. Young & L. A. Sawyer Collection)

Below right: The Greek liner *Patris*, the former *Bloemfontein Castle*, departing from Melbourne in April 1972. (Frank Andrews Collection)

in 1948, she was substituting on the Mail Service to Cape Town. A pre-war liner, she'd been built for the Round Africa service, but was temporarily reassigned to the fast mail service to the Cape while some of our other liners were still undergoing their post-war restorations. The 18-knot *Durban Castle* took a day longer, 15 days in all, than the larger ships, but otherwise was an ideal substitute. She had very comfortable accommodations for 180 in first class and 359 in tourist class. At the time, long before the tourist boom, we still carried mostly port-to-port passengers. While we carried a dance band, the remaining entertainment was arranged and organized by passenger entertainment and passenger sports committees. There was a heavy emphasis on deck games during the day and, for evenings, there was dog racing, the Ocean Derby, fancy dress, a talent show and quizzes. Ironically, passengers were not allowed to dance in the public rooms as we had a very religious chairman at the time. Instead, dancing was done along the Promenade Deck.'

Harry Andrews added, 'There was lots of competition on the East African route in those days, of course. As an alternative, we often used the British India Line, sailing out of London and taking either the *Kenya* or *Uganda*. We'd sail to Gibraltar, Marseilles, Port Said, transit the Suez Canal, Aden, Mombasa, Tanga, Zanzibar, Dar-es-Salaam, Beira and Durban. From there, we sometimes took one of two other British India passenger ships, the *Kampala* and *Karanja*, on business trips over to the Seychelles. All of these were old-style, quite elegant, very quiet passenger ships – the perfect "tonic" for our continuous, often long-distance travels. In first class, the British India liners were probably our very best favorites. Their ships were very charming, friendly and cozy. It was an era of long-serving Goanese stewards in starched white jackets and ritual afternoon teas, overhead fans and mounted elephant tusks in the main lounge.'

'Sometimes, we also travelled in the Italian-flag Lloyd Triestino liners – in ships such as the *Africa* and *Europa*', added Andrews. 'They were the most modern ships on the African runs in the 1950s, and were also the best appointed. Years ahead of any other passenger ship firms of the time, these twin liners were completely air-conditioned. I can assure you that such an amenity was a great relief, especially when docked in the likes of Beira, where humid, mid-afternoon temperatures soared over 110 degrees.'

John Havers recalled, 'On the East Africa run, Lloyd Triestino was considered to have the finest ships in the 1950s. They had the very modern, fully air-conditioned sisters *Africa* and *Europa*. They were the sensations, the preferred ships. Some British travelers actually took the train to and from Venice or Trieste just to sail in them. They were far superior to our more conservative, un-air conditioned Union-Castle ships. We used to call the Italian ships "the ice cream carts" because of their smart, all-white, blue-trimmed exteriors. Otherwise and noted for their fine service in first class, British India to East Africa was the second choice. Union-Castle was actually the third choice.'

Harry Andrews was aboard the *Durban Castle*, on a voyage from Walvis Bay to Cape Town, and recalled the murder of British passenger Gaye Gibson. 'It all made rather sensational headline news, especially since her body had been pushed through a porthole', he recalled.

'Gay Gibson was a 21-year-old actress, who had an affair with one of the stewards aboard the *Durban Castle*,' added Charles Darnell, a Union-Castle dance instructor and performer. 'He was caught, [but he had] murdered her and then tried to push the body out through the porthole. The body was never found, but the steward was later found guilty. He was given a life sentence, but later paroled and then assaulted two children.'

By the early 1960s, as rampant decolonization coupled with strengthening competition from airlines, the East African trade in particular faded – and then faded very quickly. The *Durban Castle* was withdrawn in April 1962 and quickly sold for demolition, being scrapped at Hamburg.

Left: The handsome looking *Kenya Castle*. (Robert Pabst Collection)

Right: Another view of the 552-passenger *Kenya Castle*. (Union-Castle Line)

PRETORIA CASTLE/WARWICK CASTLE

The *Warwick Castle*, sister ship to the aforementioned *Durban Castle*, was the second Union-Castle liner to be restored after war service. She had been the *Pretoria Castle*, completed in 1939, but was renamed during her reconditioning in 1946 so as to free the name *Pretoria Castle* and pleasing the South African Government for the far larger mail ship then under construction.

The *Warwick Castle* had a rather unusual wartime career – she was bought outright by the Admiralty in 1942, cut down and rebuilt as an escort aircraft carrier, capable of handling up to fifteen aircraft. She was actually the largest escort carrier then in the British fleet. She was re-purchased by Union-Castle in 1946, sent back to her Harland & Wolf builders and restored as a passenger ship. Built initially for the Round Africa service, the 17,387-grt *Warwick Castle* was first used, to help out

with pressing demands, on the express run to the Cape. She resumed sailing from Southampton in March 1947, two months after the *Capetown Castle's* first sailing.

Cruises were not part of Union-Castle's normal schedules, especially just after the war. Because of reshuffling of ships, however, the *Warwick Castle* made two cruises – fourteen-night voyages from London to Gibraltar, Casablanca, Las Palmas and Madeira, and then return to Southampton – in December and January 1951–52. A few cruises were offered in subsequent years, but not as a full, regular schedule until the arrival of the *Reina Del Mar* in 1964.

As trade declined in the 1960s, the *Warwick Castle* was retired in June 1962 and rather quickly sold to Spanish shipbreakers and ended her days at Barcelona.

Above left: The *Rhodesia Castle* after being modernized and refitted in the early 1960s. (Union-Castle Line)

Above right: The *Braemar Castle* shown off the Tilbury Landing Stage at London. (Kenneth Wightman, courtesy of Mick Lindsay)

Far left: A passenger accommodation plan from the *Rhodesia Castle* dated 1961. (Andrew Kilk Collection)

Left: An entertainment program from the *Kenya Castle* dated 9 February 1966. (Author's Collection)

DRAKENSBURG CASTLE

A short mention of the cargo ship fleet that Union-Castle also maintained is warranted. Some ships also carried up to twelve passengers. Just as the Second World War ended, in 1945, the company added five new, 8,300-grt refrigerated cargo ships – the *Riebeeck Castle, Rustenburg Castle, Rowallan Castle, Richmond Castle* and *Roxburgh Castle*. It was, in fact, the *Roxburgh Castle* that officially re-opened the Cape Mail Service in January 1947. These ships joined two pre-war ships of this type, the *Roslin Castle* and *Rochester Castle*. These ships were for the fruit trade, which was expanding rapidly – there were 320 boxes of grapes onboard the *Grantully Castle* in 1880 and this soared to 13,000,000 packages by 1972. At that time, in 1945, there was also one aged general freighter, the 1921-built *Sandown Castle*, and the *Rovuma,* a small coaster based at Beira, in the company's fleet. In 1948, the company acquired another freighter, the *Empire Duchess*, which became the *Braemar Castle*. That same year, to add to their cargo services, Union-Castle bought a controlling interest in the King Line. In 1957, two more fruit ships were added – the *Rotherwick Castle* and *Rothesay Castle*.

Renewal of the freight division was as important in ways as the restoration and rebuilding of the passenger arm. So, and under the British Government's post-war Ship Disposal Scheme, Union-Castle was able to acquire a trio of large, comparatively fast (15 knots) cargo liners. Each was built toward the very end of the war and were no longer urgently needed for military service, but instead for the resumption of commercial trading.

The 475-ft long *Empire Allenby* was purchased in 1946 and became the *Drakensburg Castle* and was fitted with austerity quarters for up to thirty-six passengers. This 9,900-grt ship was not assigned to UK service, however, but on Union-Castle's New York–South Africa run. Uniquely at the time, she and a sister, the *Good Hope Castle,* were placed under a contracted agreement with the South African Government and thereby sailed under the South African flag. They were in fact registered not in a British port, but at Cape Town.

The *Drakensburg Castle* finished her days in 1959, out in the Far East – in the hands of Hong Kong breakers.

Peter Rushton served as a cadet and later officer on several of the company's subsequent cargo vessels. 'The *Tintagel Castle* was a 9,000-grt general cargo ship built in 1955. She carried lots of cargo along with twelve passengers in very comfortable quarters. She was used at the time [in 1955] on the Round Africa run and also called at Ascension and St Helena. We often had very varied cargos. On one voyage, we loaded five live rhinos in crates at Mombasa. They were bound for the UK. One died from the heat in the Red Sea, however, and it had to be buried at sea. The ship's derricks were rigged. The dead rhino was very bloated, however, and so we tied bricks to the corpse. On another occasion, we had wild pigs, also in crates. One broke loose at Genoa and excited many screaming Italian dockers!'

'On another occasion, we had a caged cheetah on deck', added Rushton. 'It broke loose and in the fierce heat of the Red Sea no less. It dove into the sea. It took six crewmen to later rescue it.'

Peter Rushton also served on the company's well known 'fruit boats'. 'They were good-looking ships, all motor ships and had lavender hulls. They did not carry passengers, however. They had names beginning with R – so we had the *Rowallan Castle*, *Richmond Castle*, *Rustenberg Castle* and the *Roslin Castle*, which was the smallest and oldest. I was in the *Roxburgh Castle*, which sailed empty from the UK down to South Africa. On the two-week voyage, we did extensive cleaning of the holds. We had to 'de-rat' them. We called at the usual ports – Cape Town, Durban, East London and Port Elizabeth – and carried citrus fruits as well as pears and apples.'

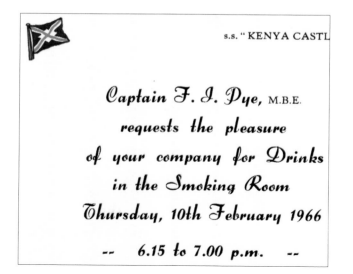

s.s. " KENYA CASTL

Captain F. I. Dye, M.B.E.

requests the pleasure

of your company for Drinks

in the Smoking Room

Thursday, 10th February 1966

-- 6.15 to 7.00 p.m. --

M.V. WARWICK CASTLE

CHILDREN'S EVENING MEAL

Cereal

Cream Soup

Fillets of Halibut Hôtelière

Minced Lamb and Spaghetti

Eggs to Order

Roast Mutton, Mint Sauce

Roast and Mashed Potatoes

Garden Peas

Cold

York Ham   Ox Tongue

Salad in Season

Sweets

Peaches and Cream

Cream Ices

Fairy Cakes   Assorted Sandwiches

Hot and Cold Milk   Orangeade

Fresh Fruit

Tuesday, February 6. 1962

UNION - CASTLE   LINE   B.537.3.60

PROGRAMME OF EVENTS

Wednesday, 9th February
a.m.   *Depart CAPE TOWN*
8.30 p.m.   *1st Sitting - Cinema—" Topkapi"*
9.00 p.m.   *Tombola*

Thursday, 10th
6.15 p.m.   *Captain's Cocktail Party*
9.00 p.m.   *Gala Dance*

Friday, 11th
10.30 a.m.   *Commence 1st rounds of Tournaments*
5.00 p.m.   *Discussion Group*
8.45 p.m.   *Tombola*
9.00 p.m.   *2nd Sitting - Cinema—" Topkapi "*

Saturday, 12th
10.30 a.m.   *Adults' Aquatic Sports*
2.30 p.m.   *Children's Cinema Show*
4.30 p.m.   *Cricket Practice*
4.30 p.m.   *Whist Drive*
9.00 p.m.   *" Kenya Castle " Ocean Derby*

Sunday, 13th
4.30 p.m.   *Cricket Match—Passengers v. Officers*
8.30 p.m.   *1st Sitting - Cinema—" Jungle Cat "*
9.00 p.m.   *Quiz*

Monday, 14th
4.30 p.m   *Return Cricket Match*
9.00 p.m.   *Dog Racing followed by Dancing*

Tuesday, 15th
10.30 a.m.   *Crossing The Line Ceremony*
8.45 p.m.   *Quiz*
9.00 p.m.   *2nd Sitting - Cinema—" Jungle Cat "*

Wednesday, 16th
10.30 a.m.   *Children's Deck Sports*
9.00 p.m.   *Frog Racing*

Thursday, 17th
4.30 p.m.   *Children's Fancy Dress Parade and Tea Party*
8.30 p.m.   *1st Sitting - Cinema—" The Rebel "*
9.00 p.m.   *Tombola*

Friday, 18th
9.00 p.m.   *Fancy Dress Dance and Cabaret*

Saturday, 19th
2.30 p.m.   *Children's Cinema Show*
8.30 p.m.   *Tombola*
9.00 p.m.   *2nd Sitting - Cinema—" The Rebel "*

Sunday, 20th
Call LAS PALMAS
9.00 p.m.   *Dancing*

Monday, 21st
8.30 p.m.   *Cinema, 1st Sitting—" The Guns Of Navarone "*
9.00 p.m   *Whist Drive*

Tuesday, 22nd
8.30 p.m.   *Whist Drive*
9.00 p.m.   *2nd Sitting - Cinema—" The Guns of Navarone "*

Wednesday, 23rd
5.30 p.m.   *Presentation of Prizes*
9.00 p.m.   *Farewell Dance*

Thursday, 24th
Arrive LONDON

Competitors in Deck Tournaments are requested to assemble at the Sports Notice Board daily at 10 a.m. & 4.15 p.m. to locate their Partners & Opponents

This Programme is Provisional and Subject to Alteration

Passengers are requested not to reserve seats at Cinema Shows by leaving books, personal belongings, etc., on the chairs

UNION-CASTLE

Fares & Sailings

SOUTH AFRICA
EAST AFRICA
ROUND AFRICA

OCTOBER, 1957
All previous issues cancelled

UNION-CASTLE

PASSAGE TICKET

IMMIGRATION OFFICER
(44)
EMBARKED
23 DEC 1965
LONDON

YOUR ATTENTION IS DRAWN TO THE CONDITIONS OF CONTRACT PRINTED INSIDE THIS TICK

Above: The cover of a passage ticket from the *Kenya Castle* and dated January 1965. (Author's Collection)

Left: The colorful sailing schedule from October 1957. (Andrew Kilk Collection).

M.V. "WARWICK CASTLE" (17,387 TONS).

Above: A baggage tag. (Author's Collection)

Right: A menu cover from the *Warwick Castle* dated February 1961. (Author's Collection)

Extract from the Log of m.v. " Warwick Castle"

Voyage 72   Cape Town to London

CAPTAIN A. E. F. PAYNE

Date	Day's Run	Lat. & Long.	Air & Sea Temp.		Wind	Remarks
Jan. 17	87	32.42S 17.28E	71	62	SW 4	Moderate following sea and swell. V/l rolling. Cloudy, fine and clear. 7 a.m. Departed Capetown.
„ 18	438	25.58S 14.14E	67	59	S 5	Rough following sea, moderate swell. V/l rolling. Cloudy, fine and clear. 11 p.m. Arrived Walvis Bay.
„ 19	196	At Walvis Bay	65	-	E 2	O'cast and clear. 1 p.m. Departed Walvis Bay.
„ 20	418	20.33S 07.30E	79	70	SSE 4	Moderate sea & swell. V/l rolling, cloudy, fine & clear.
„ 21	456	17.56S 00.01W	78	72	SSE 3	Moderate sea & swell. V/l rolling, mainly o'cast & clear.
„ 22	353	At St. Helena	78	-	SSE 2	Slight sea, low swell, cloudy, fine, and clear. 6 a.m. Arrived St. Helena. V/l Departed St. Helena midnight
„ 23	216	13.27S 08.24W	78	74	SE 3	Slight sea, low swell, mainly o'cast and clear.
„ 24	438	08.30S 13.50W	79	79	SSE 3	Slight sea, low swell, mainly fine and clear. 3.20 p.m. Arrived Ascension. 5.30 p.m. Departed Ascension.
„ 25	368	02.44S 15.35W	82	82	SxE 2	Slight sea, low swell, mainly o'cast with occ' light rain. V/l crossed Equator at 9.18 p.m.
„ 26	422	04.13N 16.53W	86	82	N 2	Slight sea, mod. swell, v/l rolling. Cloudy, fine and clear.
„ 27	411	11.01N 17.39W	76	80	N 4	Moderate sea, low swell. Cloudy, fine and clear.
„ 28	391	17.32N 17.43W	69	65	NNE 4	Moderate sea, low swell, cloudy, fine & clear. 1.48 p.m. Passed Cape Verde and Port of Dakar.
„ 29	395	24.01N 16.55W	66	62	NE 5	Mod.trough sea, moderate swell, v/l pitching. Cloudy, fine and clear.
„ 30	266	At Las Palmas	65	-	E 2	Cloudy, fine and clear. 5.52 a.m. Arrived Las Palmas 1.18 p.m. Departed Las Palmas.
„ 31	388	34.20N 13.14W	66	64	Var. 1/2	Rippled sea,mod. swell, v/l pitching. Cloudy, fine & clear.
Feb. 1	402	40.44N 10.36W	59	56	SW 2	Slight sea, moderate/heavy swell, v/l rolling & pitching. O'cast with occ. drizzle. 9.33 p.m. Entered Bay of Biscay.
„ 2	397	46.48N 06.55W	54	52	NWxW 8	Very rough sea, heavy swell, v/l pitching and rolling o'cast with light rain. 8.30 p.m. Left Bay of Biscay, entered English Channal.
„ 3	354	50.29N 00.09W	48	50	NNW 4	Moderate sea and swell. O'cast with moderate visibilty.
„ 4	144	to Tilbury				E.T.A. Tilbury 6.00 a.m.

CAPETOWN TO LONDON—6540 MILES.   AVERAGE SPEED -17.15 KNOTS

M.V. " WARWICK   CASTLE "
Tourist   Class

Farewell Dinner

———

Consommé Princess
Cream of Tomato

Darne of Salmon   Shrimp Sauce

Hearts of Celery Milanaise

Fillet of Beef à la Concorde

Breast of Turkey   Cranberry Sauce

POTATOES :   Rissolee   Parsley Boiled
Brussels Sprouts

COLD
Ham
Ox-Tongue
Salad in Season

SWEETS
Souffle aux Kirsch
Fruit Salad
Vanilla Cream Ices

Coffee   Fruit

Friday, February 3, 1961

Far left: Voyage Log from the *Warwick Castle.* (Author's Collection)

Left: A dinner menu. (Author's Collection)

GOOD HOPE CASTLE

Built at Dundee as the *Empire Life*, this ship became the *Good Hope Castle* in 1946 and had slightly larger, albeit still very basic passenger quarters for up to fifty-four. On 14 July 1947, she became the very first Union-Castle ship to be transferred to South African registry. These quarters were later removed and thereafter the ship served as a cargo vessel. She endured until she was delivered to Hong Kong scrappers in July 1959.

Left: The *Kenya Castle* photographed in the English Channel. (Luis Miguel Correia Collection)

Right: The *Rhodesia Castle* arriving off Gravesend on 2 February 1957. (Kenneth Wightman, courtesy of Mick Lindsay)

Above left: Another fine view of the *Rhodesia Castle* at Gravesend, but including the tug *Vanquisher*. (Kenneth Wightman, courtesy of Mick Lindsay)

Above right: The *Braemar Castle* in a scene dated 26 March 1962. (Albert Wilhelmi Collection)

Below right: The ex-*Kenya Castle* as the rebuilt cruise ship *Amerikanis* seen off St Thomas in 1988. (Author's Collection)

KENILWORTH CASTLE

The third of these post-war 'big freighters' was the Glasgow-built *Empire Wilson*, which, like the previous two ships, joined Union-Castle in 1946. She became the *Kenilworth Castle*. She too had temporary space for passengers, up to thirty-six in all. Of these three wartime Empire class ships of the 'Standard Fast' type, the *Kenilworth Castle* had the longest career. She was not scrapped, at Kaohsiung on Taiwan, until the summer of 1967.

Sensation of the late 1950s: The impressive-looking *Pendennis Castle* at Southampton. (Albert Wilhelmi Collection)

The *Pendennis Castle* on her maiden voyage in January 1959. (Albert Wilhelmi Collection)

UNION-CASTLE R.M.S. PENDENNIS CASTLE, 28,582 *gross tons*

Left: A romantic nighttime view. (Albert Wilhelmi Collection)

Right: The *Pendennis Castle* at the New Docks on 16 August 1967. (J&C McCutcheon Collection)

UNION-CASTLE

R.M.S.
PENDENNIS
CASTLE

UNION-C STL

R.M.S.
PENDENNIS
CASTLE

REVISED 1962

PASSENGER
ACCOMMODATION

Right: The cover of a deck plan, 1959. (Andrew Kilk Collection)

Far right: A revised deck plan from 1962. (Andrew Kilk Collection)

RMS PENDENNIS CASTLE

UNION-CASTLE

PASSENGER ACCOMMODATION

RMS PENDENNIS CASTLE

UNION-CASTLE

SAFETY INFORMATION
The "PENDENNIS CASTLE", registered in Great Britain, substantially meets International Safety Standards for new ships developed in 1960 and meets the 1966 Fire Safety requirements.

Apply to your Travel Agent:—

or *UNION-CASTLE LINE OFFICES*

Far left: Yet another revised deck plan, this one dating from 1968. (Andrew Kilk Collection)

Left: Run away to the Sun! (Andrew Kilk Collection)

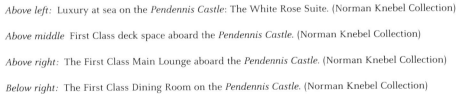

Above left: Luxury at sea on the *Pendennis Castle*: The White Rose Suite. (Norman Knebel Collection)

Above middle First Class deck space aboard the *Pendennis Castle*. (Norman Knebel Collection)

Above right: The First Class Main Lounge aboard the *Pendennis Castle*. (Norman Knebel Collection)

Below right: The First Class Dining Room on the *Pendennis Castle*. (Norman Knebel Collection)

PRETORIA CASTLE/S. A. ORANJE

'My very first assignment at Union-Castle was the *Pretoria Castle,* then brand new [she had been commissioned in July 1948]. I was on Voyage Number 6. She was on the Cape Mail Express route between Southampton, Las Palmas, Cape Town, Port Elizabeth, East London and Durban. She and her sister, the *Edinburgh Castle,* were then the best liners in the fleet and everyone, it seemed, wanted to travel in them. Passengers nearly queued-up for passages. Carrying 214 in first class and 514 in tourist class, those last-named quarters were then used by southbound British migrants. The South African Government paid £100 each toward these migrant fares for selected professionals – namely engineers, scientists and teachers. It was not quite the huge migrant scheme enacted by the Australian Government in those post-war years, but the South Africans undertook a sizeable recruitment.'

'Union-Castle was the ideal "career company" in those times, the future looked tremendous and one could expect to reach full purser's rank by their late forties or early fifties,' added John Dimmock. 'In those early years, as the lowest member of the purser's department, you had non-officer status. We were not allowed on the passenger decks and we were only allowed two bottles of beer each day!'

The 28,705-grt *Pretoria Castle* and her twin sister, the *Edinburgh Castle,* were post-war sensations to British shipbuilding and shipping – they were the largest liners, if fact the largest merchant ships, to be built since the *Queen Elizabeth* was commissioned in 1940. Special attention was given to both ships, both were said to be the finest ships yet in the Union-Castle fleet and both were solidly booked in their early years. The 747-ft long *Pretoria Castle* even had a unique, newsworthy naming. It was performed by Mrs J. C. Smuts, wife of famed Field Marshall Smuts, who was then Prime Minister of South Africa. Mrs Smuts would not travel to the Harland & Wolff shipyard at Belfast and so instead named the new liner via radio telephone from her home near Pretoria. At the press of a button, a series of electric 'impulses' went to Cape Town, then by radio to London and finally by land line to Belfast. This signal released a bottle of, quite appropriately, South African wine on the bow of the gleaming new ship and quickly sent it down the ways.

The profile of the 747-ft long *Pretoria Castle* was a moderation of the classic company mail ship – twin masts and one large, centrally-positioned, red and black funnel, a cruiser stern, a rounded forward superstructure and, of course, a lavender-colored hull. She was a strikingly handsome ship – and had accommodations for 227 in very fine first class and 478 in noticeably more comfortable tourist class as well as seven holds for large amounts of cargo. She and her sister were noteworthy within the company itself – they were the first steamships (rather than motor ships) to be built in over twenty years. The *Pretoria Castle* entered the mail service in July 1948, with the *Edinburgh Castle* following in December.

The *Pretoria Castle* was selected to represent Union-Castle on 15 June 1953 when hundreds of ships, both merchant and naval, were assembled off Spithead. The occasion was the Royal Naval Review for the coronation of Queen Elizabeth II. That same year, added to the festivity, was the centenary of Union-Castle, since its forerunner, the Union Collier Company, was formed in 1853.

As older Castle liners faded away into retirement, the *Pretoria Castle* and *Edinburgh Castle* were becoming the 'senior ships' by the early 1960s. In 1962, both had extended refits, which included the installation of what had become an almost common amenity: full air-conditioning throughout. In the spring of 1965, there were further changes to both ships – more cabins were fitted with private bathrooms while outwardly their forward masts were shortened, the aft masts removed and a new mast affixed above the wheelhouse. It was, in ways, having these twin, older liners look more like the newer *Pendennis Castle*, *Windsor Castle* and *Transvaal Castle*.

Change was in the wind! In 1965, in its own fleet expansion and in growing strength and control, Safmarine Lines took a significant hold in Union-Castle operations. They bought the three-year-old *Transvaal Castle* and the 1948-built *Pretoria Castle*. Promptly, the pair were renamed *S. A. Vaal* and *S. A. Oranje.* The sale officially took place on 31 January 1966. The *Transvaal Castle* was formally renamed on 12 January 1966; the *Pretoria Castle* just weeks later on 2 February. The ships continued to be operated by Union-Castle, however, but on bareboat charters. Both ships were repainted in Safmarine colors. In the details of the agreement, Safmarine

would operate three mail ships – the two newly purchased ships with the responsibility for eventually building a third (but which never materialized in the end). Full South African control of the two Safmarine liners was made in early 1969 and thereafter they flew the South African flag.

Earlier, in 1960, the very first Boeing 707 of South African Airways was placed on the London–Johannesburg run. Gradually, the airliner would become the victorious competitor over the classic passenger liner. But equally significant, in 1965, British & Commonwealth joined three giants in British merchant shipping – P&O, Ocean Transport & Trading and Furness Withy – in forming Overseas Containers Limited. It was the beginning of the container revolution, the great divide of cargo transport by sea, which would decisively effect Union-Castle passenger ship operations as well. The devastating, six-week British Seamen's Strike of May–June 1966 all but sealed the future fates of classic liner operations.

There were all but devastating fuel oil price increases for all ships in 1973–74. Suddenly, the Union-Castle liners had become even more expensive to operate and so, to reduce costs and consumption, an extra day was added to their schedules. But the clock was ticking. The *S. A. Oranje* was withdrawn in September 1975 and then made a cargo-only voyage to Durban before continuing out to Kaohsiung on Taiwan for scrapping. She had been on the mail run for twenty-seven years.

John Mengers served aboard the *S. A. Oranje* in the early 1970s, near the end of her days. 'She had beautiful wood paneling, perhaps more beautiful than even the later ships. But her bridge was almost primitive by then. It seemed decades behind, say, the newer *Windsor Castle*. By then well over twenty years of age, the *S. A. Oranje* and *Edinburgh Castle* had another disadvantage in their later years – they did not have stabilizers.' Jim Alford, a specialist in repairing ship's machinery, added, 'Ships like the *S. A. Oranje* and *Edinburgh Castle* were very rundown, almost neglected, in their final years. There were all sorts of problems and then assorted remedies to keep them going.'

Left: The *Pendennis Castle* created a new exterior look for the Mail Ships. (Luis Miguel Corrreia Collection)

Right: A fine view of this good-looking ship. (Robert Pabst Collection)

Right: The Southampton Docks: The outbound *QE2* with the *Pendennis Castle* to the right. (David Williams Collection)

Left: Sentimental journey: The *Pendennis Castle* departs from Cape Town on her final voyage to the UK. The date is 2 June 1976. (Luis Miguel Correia Collection)

EDINBURGH CASTLE

'Within the huge British passenger ship trade of the 1950s, seamen had preferences. For a time, I worked for Cunard and served as a waiter on the *Queen Mary*, *Ivernia* and the *Mauretania*. I earned about $8 a week in the 1950s, but tips made the differences. The New York-bound liners were the best, of course, with all the Americans aboard. They were the very best tippers. Later, I sailed on the Union-Castle liners to and from Africa, onboard ships such as the *Edinburgh Castle*. But where there were virtually no tips. The British passengers, especially down in tourist class on Union-Castle ships, rarely if ever tipped.'

'I remember taking the Boat Train down from London to the Southampton Docks and boarding the *Edinburgh Castle*,' recalled John Castlemere. 'We sailed via Las Palmas in the Canaries and then were in Cape Town in thirteen days. When going to South Africa, Union-Castle and its ships was the classic way to travel. I also remember passing the northbound liner, the *Stirling Castle*, at sea, in mid-ocean. The two ships sounded their whistles in an exciting salute. Union-Castle was all done with precision, more like a railway schedule.'

Charles and Jean Darnell were dancers, among the early shipboard entertainers, onboard the *Edinburgh Castle* (and later on the *Pendennis Castle*, *Windsor Castle* and *S. A. Vaal*). 'Beginning in 1970, we were hired to do shows, to teach dance and to socialize,' they recalled. 'Mostly, we worked in first class. It was still very formal – there was dressing for dinner on most nights. Onboard the *Edinburgh Castle* and the other Castle liners, first class was still very grand. There were lords and ladies, industrial barons, actors and actresses. We recall the likes of Harold Good, who owned the first cinema in Britain. Many took lots of luggage as well as their own cars, including Jaguars and Rolls-Royces.'

'Down in tourist class, we had mostly migrants going out and a few tourists,' added Charles Darnell. 'On the homeward trips to the UK, there were mostly South African travelers and increasingly younger South Africans. We'd have jockeys, footballers, cricketers. The South Africans themselves used the coastal voyages between Cape Town, Port Elizabeth, East London and Durban as "mini cruises" – two-week voyages that were ideal for holidays. Once, we had a full cricket team onboard. I also recall Ian Smith, the Prime Minister of Southern Rhodesia. He'd stroll the decks, use the public rooms and visit the shops but always surrounded by his bodyguards.'

In their seven years onboard Union-Castle, Charles and Jean Darnell only cancelled one performance and that was because of bad weather. 'We were hired through a talent agent in London which had been contacted by Union-Castle. We had our audition onboard at the Southampton Docks. Wearing top hats, we did Latin and ballroom dances in an otherwise empty lounge. We were hired and thereafter reviewed by both the talent agents and Union-Castle. We worked on six-week contracts with ten days off in between. We remained on the same ship in those days – there were no changes. There was no cruise director as we see today. We reported to the purser. The only other performer was an accordion player. We organized the entertainment and got the officers to join in the shows. It was all like an old music hall – varied amateur acts, some good and some not so good. We'd also have theme nights such as Scottish Night and Eights & Reel. There were other complications, however. In those years, the very powerful Seamen's Union was very much against paid professional entertainers. Once, we returned to our cabin and found that someone had put Jean's ballroom dresses in boiling hot water in the bath. They were ruined!'

The *Edinburgh Castle* outlived her sister, the *S. A. Oranje*, by just a few months. She went to the Far East for scrap in May 1976. 'We were at Southampton when the *Edinburgh Castle* sailed off to Taiwan and the breakers,' recalled Charles Darnell. 'She had only a skeleton crew and looked very sad.'

A model of the proposed design for the *Windsor Castle* from 1957. (Cronican-Arroyo Collection)

Left: Brand new: The mighty *Windsor Castle* shown in the Gladstone Dry Dock at Liverpool in the summer of 1960. (Kenneth Wightman Collection, courtesy of David Williams)

Below: The magnificent *Windsor Castle* sailing from Cape Town. (Gillespie-Faber Collection)

BLOEMFONTEIN CASTLE

'The *Bloemfontein Castle* was unique to the Union-Castle fleet when she was first commissioned in 1950. She carried only one class of passengers, 721 in all-cabin class,' noted John Dimmock, who served in her pursers' department. 'This ship was a one-off – built especially for the outward migrant trade that was to have been inspired largely by the East African groundnut scheme. There was to have been a huge flow of British workers and their families, but unfortunately this never materialized. Consequently, this ship was the "odd duckling" in our fleet. She was placed instead on a special, intermediate East African service going as far as Beira. She was, of course, an interesting experiment for Union-Castle with her one-class quarters. Her passengers did, however, tend to grade themselves – selecting their own type and style of public rooms. Some wanted the luxury bars and others the spit'n sawdust style. In addition to British passengers, we also carried Germans, Dutch and Portugese as well, and often taking the overflow from other passenger ships. In those years, the 1950s, there was still only one plane a week!'

The *Bloemfontein Castle* traded out of London and sometimes Rotterdam to Las Palmas, Lobito, Walvis Bay, Cape Town, Port Elizabeth, East London, Durban, Lourenco Marques and Beira. Her basic design was classically Union-Castle with a large, single stack, cruiser stern and rounded forward superstructure, but in a different arrangement, she had a single mast placed above the wheelhouse. All other Castle liners of that time had two masts.

John Dimmock was aboard one of the *Bloemfontein Castle's* most heroic moments. 'It was a most interesting as well as exciting adventure,' he recalled. 'We rescued the passengers and crew [116 passengers and 118 crew] from the *Klipfontein*, a passenger-cargo ship from the Holland-Africa Line, on 8 January 1953. We had just been together at Lourenço Marques and we were both racing for the single dock at Beira. Unfortunately, the *Klipfontein* ran aground and then began to break in half and sink. We received the SOS just after lunch and got to the stricken vessel by late afternoon. We managed to save everyone and everything – including a Dachshund and a canary.'

Frequent Union-Castle traveler Harry Andrews was also aboard the *Bloemfontein Castle* when she made a heroic rescue of all hands from the wrecked *Klipfontein*. 'In those days, in the late '40s and during the '50s, there was a terrific shortage of berths [pier space] in South and East African ports. Often, freighters with less priority had to wait for three or four weeks. Sometimes liners had to wait for a week. At Beira, companies couldn't book a berth in advance. The first ship to arrive was given the available berth. Consequently, the captain of the *Klipfontein* decided to clip a few miles off his voyage – and off his determined race with the *Bloemfontein Castle* – and so brought his ship very close to the shore. Subsequently, she hit a dangerous reef and was immediately ripped open. She sank in something like twelve minutes.'

The *Bloemfontein Castle* remained in the Union-Castle fleet for only nine years. Although comparatively new, she was, in the face of a gradually declining trade (migrants were her mainstay after all), made redundant. Very quickly, she was sold to the Chandris Lines (to be operated by a new subsidiary known as the Europe-Australia Line), hoisted the Greek colors and was rechristened *Patris* (for 'Homeland'). Her capacity was increased to 739 passengers and later to 1,036 (and later up to 1,400), all in one class. In this next life, she ferried immigrants from Piraeus through the Suez out to Australian ports, Fremantle, Melbourne and Sydney, and carried budget tourists on the homeward trips. She later sailed in company with such Chandris liners as the *Ellinis*, *Australis* and *Britanis*. This work for her ended in 1972 – again in face of a declining trade, but also from a losing battle with the airlines.

The *Patris* was reassigned next to cruise service out of Australia, sailing mostly up to Singapore. In 1975, she performed heroic and noble duties as a floating refuge for the homeless of Darwin, Australia. The city had nearly been destroyed in a ferocious tropical storm. A year later, with her assignment again changed, she was sent to the Adriatic Sea for ferry service (a large garage was specially installed onboard) from Ancona, Italy and then across to Patras and Piraeus in Greece. In 1979, she changed hands for a third time – being sold by Chandris to another Greek operator, the Karageorgis Lines, who renamed her *Mediterranean Island* and then, in 1981, *Mediterranean Star*. Her very last role seems to have been a ferry service between Venice and Alexandria.

After some time in lay-up in Greek waters, she was sold, in 1987, to a Caribbean-based intermediary firm, temporarily renamed *Terra* and then delivered to ship breakers at Gadani Beach in Pakistan.

Above: The 783-ft long *Windsor Castle* had a powerful, imposing appearance. (Luis Miguel Correia Collection)

Right: The new flagship at the Southampton Docks in the early 1960s. (David Williams Collection)

Along the Southampton Docks. The *Winchester Castle* and then the *Pretoria Castle* are behind. (Albert Wilhelmi Collection)

Departing from East London. (Albert Wilhelmi Collection)

In Durban harbor. (Albert Wilhelmi Collection)

Another view at Durban. (Albert Wilhelmi Collection)

RHODESIA CASTLE

The still popular and profitable Round Africa service needed reinforcement as well as renewal by the early 1950s. Several aged, pre-war liners on this run were soon to be retired. Union-Castle designers and engineers went to work and took the plans of the previous *Bloemfontein Castle*, created slightly smaller ships, returned to the twin-mast design and created them as more appealing, all-cabin class ships. 'They were the "new stars" in the fleet,' recalled John Dimmock. 'They were mini versions of the very popular *Pretoria Castle* and *Edinburgh Castle*. They had added, improved amenities – such as air-conditioned dining rooms for almost 300.'

All built by a longtime friend and business ally, Harland & Wolff Ltd, the *Rhodesia Castle* came first, being commissioned in October 1951. The *Kenya Castle* followed a few months later, in February 1952. Finally, the *Braemar Castle* arrived in November 1952, therein completing the company's six-liner post-war rebuilding program. Hereafter, and for several years to come, the Round Africa service was programmed, with alternating departures from London, as: the *Kenya Castle*, *Dunnottar Castle* and *Durban Castle* going outwards via Suez and the East Coast; the *Rhodesia Castle*, *Braemar Castle* and *Warwick Castle* in reverse, using the West Coast. There were sailings twice a month, one in each direction.

'The Union-Castle passenger ships, while always the largest and perhaps best known in African service, were never quite as good as the British India liners and certainly were surpassed by the Lloyd Triestino ships on the East African run,' according to Harry Andrews. 'However, when Union-Castle refitted [in the early 1960s] the likes of the *Rhodesia Castle* and her two sisters – their best "Round Africa" ships – they were much better and made all cabin class, which was actually equal to first class.'

There was a premature end to it all, however. The fifty-year-old regular Round Africa service ended in the spring 1962. Business was declining – and rapidly so. The *Rhodesia Castle* and her two sisters were the last survivors on this trade and were assigned to a modified, restyled service: London to Gibraltar, Genoa, Port Said, Suez, Aden, Mombasa, Zanzibar, Dar es Salaam, Beira and then turnaround at Beira – returning via the same ports as well as varying calls at Lourenço Marques, Tanga, Naples and Marseilles. The entire voyage took some thirty-three days. Passengers could, however, and as Union-Castle advertised, still make a full circumnavigation of Africa by connecting with one of the mail ships at Durban.

In 1966, after the *Braemar Castle* was withdrawn, the enduring *Rhodesia Castle* and *Kenya Castle* were teamed briefly with two onetime competitors,

British India's *Kenya* and *Uganda*. 'By 1966–67, we all knew the company was running down,' recalled John Dimmock. 'Inevitably, even the big mail ships would eventually go. It was all just a matter of time.'

The *Rhodesia Castle* arrived at the London Docks on 4 May 1967, concluding the final East African voyage. The Round Africa service was officially over. She was soon sent off to the River Blackwater to await a possible sale. There were no buyers, however. As the lead ship of this trio, she was delivered to scrappers out on Taiwan in October 1967. She was only sixteen years old.

Above: A sitting room in a First Class suite aboard the *Windsor Castle.* (Norman Knebel Collection)

Right: A splendid poster of the new *Windsor Castle.* (Albert Wilhelmi Collection)

Above left: Windsor Castle: A three-berth cabin in Tourist Class. (Norman Knebel Collection)

Above right: Windsor Castle: The Tourist Class Smoking Room. (Norman Knebel Collection)

KENYA CASTLE

The second of this threesome had, in a twist of fate, the longest career of all. She endured for forty-nine years, until scrapped in 2001. Commissioned in November 1952, the last of the three new Round Africa sisters, the *Kenya Castle* was decommissioned after a comparatively short career in the spring of 1967. Laid up in the River Blackwater, she was fortunate to find a buyer – Greece's then fast-growing Chandris Lines. Taken to Greece, extensively rebuilt and renamed *Amerikanis* ('American Lady'), she was intended to be a two-class trans-Atlantic liner, sailing between the Mediterranean and New York. But the age of crossing was then in rapid decline and so plans soon changed – carrying 910 all-first class passengers, she would be used in year-round cruising, mostly from New York. In the 1970s, she moved to summer season European cruising, in Scandinavian and Mediterranean waters, and later was chartered to Costa Line (and was even repainted in their colors) from 1980 until 1984. Afterward, she resumed Chandris cruising until she was laid-up in 1999 and sold for scrapping two years later.

Right: A deck plan dated 1960. (Andrew Kilk Collection)

Far right: An updated deck plan dated 1973. (Andrew Kilk Collection)

UNION-CASTLE

R.M.S. WINDSOR CASTLE

PASSENGER ACCOMMODATION

UNION-CASTLE
SAFMARINE

RMS WINDSOR CASTLE

PASSENGER ACCOMMODATION

Left: Passing The Bluff at Durban. (Albert Wilhelmi Collection)

Windsor Castle on her Maiden Voyage.   EIAY

Right: A maiden voyage view at Southampton. (Albert Wilhelmi Collection)

BRAEMAR CASTLE

'I recall the captain of the *Braemar Castle*, during a sailing in the Red Sea, when he was convinced he'd seen a UFO,' recalled Harry Andrews. 'Supposedly sighted at 3 in the morning, he was, however, reluctant to send a message to the London home office. It seems he didn't want to disturb his chances of being appointed commodore.'

Mike Howe went to sea in 1963, aged sixteen, in the twilight of the great British merchant navy. There were some 6,000 ships in the nation's merchant fleet back then and some 35,000 men and women manning them, but it was all fading fast: rising costs, unionization and fierce competition from less expensive Third World shipping lines. "

'I remember the great King George V Docks in London and, being so busy, where ships were docked two abreast. It is now gone, replaced partially by London City Airport. Only some of the old sailor and docker pubs are still there, mostly in Silvertown and near the Tate & Lyle sugar refinery. As a teenage boy, I had to report to the Shipping Federation office in Leman Street near Whitechapel in East London. It was a grim area, Jack-the-Ripper territory. The Federation placed you on a ship and that was my beginning.'

Mike soon found his way on to the *Braemar Castle*, a very moderate liner by today's standards of only 17,000 tons and carrying a mere 550 passengers. 'I was a deck boy and had to rise at 4 in the morning,' he recalled. 'We worked with "holy stones," stones with a wood handle, and using sand and something called Atlas Grease Killer, and then we sanded down the teak decks. We worked in all kinds of weather until 7 a.m., when the passengers began to awake. The decks were always inspected and had to be sparkling white, and then we hosed them down. I later became a deck hand and then an AB, an Able Bodied Seaman.'

The *Braemar Castle* was used on the very long Round Africa service. 'They were four-month roundtrips, sailing from London to the Suez, Aden and ports all along East Africa. It was all very British still and all very colonial and all very classist and even racist. There was absolutely no direct interaction with "coloreds" in South Africa then, which horrified me because I believed firmly in equality. Our passengers were the last of the "Empire builders", people all traveling with a purpose and maybe some slight immigration, but barely any tourism as we know it today. South Africa still wanted to increase its white population and so some Brits were lured there, to a new life. It was of course all soon to change, by the end of the '60s. It seemed, however, that behind the scenes onboard the ship, every crewman had a scam going. I'd give a galley cook $3 and he'd serve passenger food to me – and for the next four months! It was the most magnificent food, of course. Another, a laundryman, did all my washing, whites as well as work clothes, for $1. They were returned in beautiful condition.'

By the late 1960s, Mike had turned to freighters, seeing the world and making money, but 'turning the corner', as he said. The great British fleet was in steady and very rapid decline. Later becoming a building surveyor, his days at sea provided 'great memories', he concluded.

The East African passenger run fell away by the mid-1960s. There was tremendous de-colonization which abruptly ended the steady flow of many passengers, coupled with the rising operating costs for British-flag passenger ships, and all while cargos began to go instead to newly created, nationalistic African shipping companies. Union-Castle pulled out of East African service by 1967 and British India two years later. Lloyd Triestino actually stayed the longest, until the early 1970s. These days, ports such as Mombasa and Durban are visited by modern cruise liners, carrying tourists on all-first class leisure voyages.

Sawyer & Mitchell in *The Cape Run* wrote, 'On the East Coast and in Central Africa, the political wind of change which had started as a gentle breeze in the late 1950s was beginning to blow much stronger at the turn of the decade.' Country after country opted for independence. Many of these were very significant to Union-Castle. Kenya and Zanzibar became self-governed in 1963, as examples, and Northern Rhodesia a year later. 'The colonial trade, literally commuting on home leaves were a great part of our business,' noted John Dimmock. 'Suddenly, it seemed, they were all gone. Our ships on the East African run were quite empty.'

'The East African service was also killed by sheer economics. There was decolonization, but also the closing of the Suez Canal,' recalled Peter Rushton. 'In the face of a very diminished trade, it had become complicated and far too expensive.'

The *Braemar Castle* was the first and ironically the youngest of this threesome to be retired. She stopped sailing at the end of 1965 and, while some thought was given to refitting her as a fulltime cruise ship, costs were rising. The idea was abandoned. The *Braemar Castle* was sold to breakers in Scotland in early 1966. She was just over thirteen years old.

Above left: Departure from Cape Town. (Albert Wilhelmi Collection)

Above right: End of an era: Final departure from Southampton in the summer of 1977. (Union-Castle Line)

Below right: Farewell: The *Margarita L* is seen departing Southampton Water in the fall of 1977. (David Williams Collection)

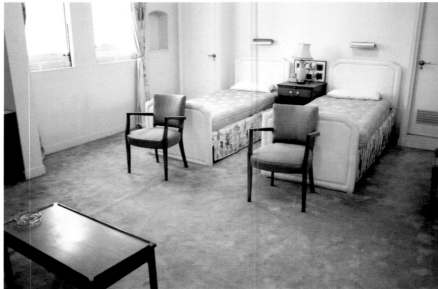

Left: The *Margarita L.* ex-*Windsor Castle*, laid-up in Greece. (Antonio Scrimali Collection)

Right: The Magnolia Suite aboard the laid-up *Margarita L.* photographed on 14 December 1998. (Peter Knego Collection)

Right: Hotel Class to South Africa: Inaugural of the new *Transvaal Castle* in 1962. (Albert Wilhelmi Collection)

Below: Out of work: The *Margarita L.* and another Latsis Line passenger ship, the *Marianna 9* (ex-*Principe Perfeito*), as seen in December 1998. (Peter Knego Collection)

PENDENNIS CASTLE

'My earliest remembrance of travelling by sea was in the 1950s when I accompanied my parents out to South Africa in the ships of the Union-Castle Line,' recalled Howard Franklin, who later became a shipboard lecturer. 'These trips continued on a fairly regular basis into the 1960s and during the British winters. Union-Castle ships left Southampton at 4 o'clock on a Thursday afternoon for the thirteen-day voyage via Las Palmas to Cape Town. While the majority of the passengers disembarked at Cape Town, we always remained in the ship for its onward passage via Port Elizabeth and East London to Durban, where we always stayed at the famous Edward Hotel, located on Marine Parade, North Beach. The sea voyage saw the same families travelling each year. We sailed on the *Pendennis Castle* and also often sailed on the *Windsor Castle* with Captain A. Hort. The chief purser was normally the jovial John Dimmock, who also took care of my Mother's jewellery. There were only 200 or so berths in first class and my parents dressed formally for dinner each evening apart from sailing day and Sunday, both of which were informal. Children didn't go to dinner as we had our own High Tea, which was served in the late afternoon.'

'Union-Castle ships were designated Mail Ships,' remembered Franklin. 'Their most famous and frequent passenger was Princess Alice, Countess of Athlone. She was married to Prince Alexander of Teck, who became Earl of Athlone, a former Governor General of South Africa. Princess Alice travelled with her lady-in-waiting, Miss Joan Lascelles, and departed Britain in January and returning to her home at Kensington Palace, London in April. In South Africa, she more often than not stayed with Mr and Mrs Gardner Williams at their beautiful estate Vergenoeg, which was in Muizenburg on the Cape Peninsula.'

'Our return journey from Durban to Southampton was via Capetown and Las Palmas,' concluded Franklin. 'We sailed on a Tuesday, normally in the *Pendennis Castle*. Captain R. Cambridge was in command and the Chief Purser was Mr D. Myerscough, who I remember as a very formal man.'

Earlier, in 1955, rumors were brisk that P&O was to buy Union-Castle. Business seemed assured – and profitable – as the South African Government had just signed a renewed mail contract, extending for ten years beginning from January 1 1957. The finances are sometimes curious, often unpredictable, however, and such that Union-Castle merged instead with another important British shipowner, the Clan Line, in October 1955. P&O was out. The two lines were then merged into a single holding company – British & Commonwealth Shipping Company Limited. It all became completely official as of 31 January 1956. Fleets were strengthened, crews became inter-changeable and all while there was a link to an airline (Hunting & Son) and a mail ship replacement program for Union-Castle. The Clan Line, with such holdings as the Houston Line and Scottish Shire Line, had fifty-seven ships; Union-Castle combined with its holdings had forty-two ships. The British merchant navy was still very much the largest anywhere, even if only for another few years.

'After the merger, Union-Castle and Clan Line officers became interchangeable,' recalled Peter Rushton. 'The scope was vast and also included Scottish Tankers, Springbok Line (which was South African), Bullard & King, the King Line and Bowater Paper Company. Later, Safmarine Lines was integrated as well. Clan Line ships became Safmarine ships – such as the *Clan Sutherland*, which changed to *S. A. Statesman*. Also some Clan ships went over to Union-Castle. It had all changed – some passenger crews from the big mail ships might go to, say, a tanker in Persian Gulf service. There were shocks all around!'

'Officers from freighters would suddenly be transferred to the liners and need full dress rigs,' added Rushton. 'Of course, some of the personalities didn't fit either. These officers were suddenly expected to be social and do dining and dancing. They'd have to rotate between first and tourist class, but clearly preferred first class. The passenger ships were policed by masters-of-arms, who watched everything and who had great power. You could not be caught, say, with a woman. There was absolutely no fraternization. In fact, the officers didn't even fraternize very much with the crew. There were two different worlds. Even some passenger ships – Shaw Savill's *Dominion Monarch* and Royal Mail Lines' *Highland Monarch* and *Amazon* classes – had separate superstructures for this very reason. Company managers and superintendents believed that familiarity bred contempt.'

The *Pendennis Castle* represented a 'new generation' at Union-Castle. Some thought she was a splendid ship, a grand continuation of the past; others found her too modern, too plastic and some even referred to her as the 'formica palace'. Built at Belfast, the 28,000-tonner – with a long, sleek appearance, domed funnel and single mast above her wheelhouse – was commissioned on New Year's Day 1959. She set off for the Cape. She was the first Castle liner to be fitted with fin stabilizers, a feature added during construction and which caused her to be lengthened (while still on the slipway at Harland & Wolff) from 748 to 763 feet in length. Her quarters were arranged for 167 in first class and 475 in tourist plus twenty-two interchangeable depending upon demand. For cargo, she was typical of Union-Castle mail ships – she had seven holds.

Typically, the *Pendennis Castle* was a very fast ship (over twenty-two knots) and it had long been planned to reduce the Cape Mail Express from eight to seven ships and reduce the passage time between Southampton and Cape Town from 13½ to 11½ days. In the summer of 1965, this acceleration took hold – the *Stirling Castle* made the final Thursday afternoon 4 o'clock sailing on 8 July; the following week, on Friday, 16 July at 1 o'clock, the *Windsor Castle* cast off from Southampton.

The *Pendennis Castle* endured for seventeen years before being withdrawn in June 1976, by then leaving only the *Windsor Castle* and *S. A. Vaal* to maintain the much withered passenger services. Service to the Cape was now also maintained by chartered freighters, such as Blue Star Line's *Andalucia Star*, which were repainted in Union-Castle colors. Meanwhile, the *Pendennis Castle* was sold to the Ocean Queen Navigation Company, based in the Philippines, but using Panamanian registry. She was renamed *Ocean Queen*, but did little more than sit at anchorage in Hong Kong harbor. She changed hands again, in 1977, going to Kinvarra Bay Shipping Company and becoming the *Sinbad* and then *Sinbad I*. Again, she never sailed, however, until taken to Kaohsiung on Taiwan in April 1980 for breaking-up.

R.M.S. "Transvaal Castle"

Above: Fine lines: The handsome *Transvaal Castle* was the last of the big Mail Ships. (Albert Wilhelmi Collection)

Left: Preparing for the maiden voyage, at Southampton in January 1962. (Union-Castle Line)

Nighttime at Cape Town. (Albert Wilhelmi Collection)

At Southampton, November 1964. (Albert Wilhelmi Collection)

Maiden voyage departure from Cape Town, 2 February 1962. (Albert Wilhelmi Collection)

Left: At Southampton. (Union-Castle Line).

Above: The *S. A. Vaal* in her final year of South African service. (Luis Miguel Correia Collection)

Right: A deck plan dated 1976. (Andrew Kilk Collection)

GOOD HOPE CASTLE & SOUTHAMPTON CASTLE

Sue Mengers worked aboard the Swan Hellenic Cruises' *Ankara*, a chartered Turkish passenger ship that cruised the Mediterranean from end to end. 'The Cayzer family, eight of them, came aboard for a summer cruise in 1966,' she recalled. 'They worked in London for most of the year, but cruised in summer. Myself, I wanted a better job. I met one of them, told him and he replied "My uncle has a shipping line!"' She and her future husband John soon joined Union-Castle.

'There were three Cayzer brothers – Sir Nicholas, Sir Bernard and Sir Anthony. Bernard looked after the passenger ships,' added Sue. 'My husband John had actually done some service with the Clan Line. He was soon sent to the *Good Hope Castle* and *Southampton Castle*, terrifically fast freighters on the run to the South African Cape. They were among the fastest cargo liners in the world – they did up to 26–27 knots at times! Onboard, as third purser, he was paid £60 a month on a freighter and £80 a month on a liner.'

In 1965, Union-Castle accelerated its mail ship services and reduced its Cape-bound fleet to five liners and two high-speed freighters. 'These cargo liners, the *Good Hope Castle* and *Southampton Castle*, were known as the "mini mails",' noted John Dimmock. 'They were later fitted with twelve passenger berths, an alteration underwritten by the British Government as they alone called at remote Ascension and St Helena. Their visits were among the very few links with Britain.'

'In addition to cargo, we carried deck passengers – mostly workers – on overnight trips onboard the *Southampton Castle* and *Good Hope Castle*,' added John Mengers. 'There might be fifty or sixty of them. We had, of course, our twelve cabin passengers, which were mostly older travelers. But sometimes we had young girls, who wanted a quiet voyage, a bit of a change.'

High drama! On 29 June 1973, the *Good Hope Castle* was reported to be ablaze, burning, listing and abandoned near Ascension Island. Her eighty-two passengers and crew later spent thirty-six hours in lifeboats before being rescued by an American tanker. Coincidentally, the *Southampton Castle* was nearby while the *Good Hope Castle* was reportedly 'burning furiously', with her bridge front collapsed. An aft-deck cargo of drums had exploded, the sacks of mail were burning and her accommodation was gutted. A gale didn't help matters. It was not until 7 July that a salvage tug arrived; a rescue team was able to board the ship and reported that the ship was badly damaged and some decks had buckled. With continued smoldering fires, the ship was finally placed under tow – she was intended to go to Dakar, but then was refused entry and then rerouted to Las Palmas, but refused again. Finally, she was towed all the way to Antwerp, where she finally arrived on 18 August. Inspections revealed that her hull and machinery were still in good condition and full repairs, including 1,000 tons of steel, followed in a Spanish shipyard at Bilbao. Fully restored, she resumed Southampton–Cape sailings in May 1974.

As the mail ship service ended, and in the increasingly efficient container ship age, these sisters were laid-up in 1977 after only twelve years of Union-Castle service. Both found buyers, however, and were sold in February 1978 to Italy's Costa Line. The *Southampton Castle* became the *Franca C*; the *Good Hope Castle* changed to *Paola C*. Their names were later amended to *Franca Costa* and *Paola Costa*, and both ships were employed in the Italy–South America service. But again, and in the expanding container ship era, their days were numbered. The ex-*Southampton Castle* was handed over to Shanghai breakers in January 1984; the former *Good Hope Castle* followed that June.

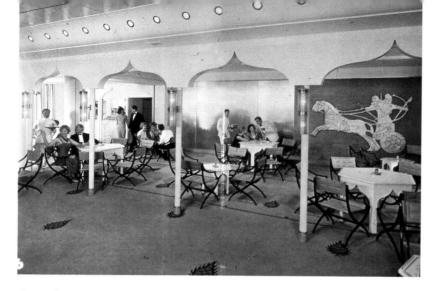

The Garden Room aboard the *S. A. Vaal*. (Norman Knebel Collection)

The Orangery, a popular bar, on the *S. A. Vaal*. (Norman Knebel Collection)

The sitting room of a suite onboard the *S. A. Vaal*. (Norman Knebel Collection)

The Dining Room aboard the one-class *S. A. Vaal*. (Norman Knebel Collection)

Left: Farewell to Cape Town. (Albert Wilhelmi Collection)

Right: A moodful view. (Albert Wilhelmi Collection)

WINDSOR CASTLE

In January 2003, the first meeting of the so-called *RMS Windsor Castle* Foundation was held in Southampton. The famed ship had been in Greek hands since 1977 and had been laid-up for the previous decade. Strong rumor was that the liner was to go to scrap. Preservationists wanted to save one of Britain's last great ocean liners. Being a partial museum was included in the plan by the group.

Union-Castle celebrated the centenary of its association with the port of Southampton in 1957. That same year, in December, there seemed a most fitting event – the company laid the keel for its largest liner yet and for continued Southampton–South Africa service. To be named *Windsor Castle*, the 36,123-grt ship would be built by Cammell Laird at Birkenhead and would rank as the largest British-flag liner since the *Queen Elizabeth* in 1940, the largest ever to be built in England and the largest to be created on the Mersey. Shortly afterward, another big liner, the *Pendennis Castle,* was to be launched. The future seemed bright – and almost unending.

The 783ft-long *Windsor Castle* was a mighty, powerful looking ship and a refinement of the earlier *Pendennis Castle*. She could carry 782 passengers – 191 in a very fine first class and 591 in a more comfortable tourist class. With these new liners, Union-Castle was realizing, and more and more, that tourists were traveling as well as passengers on holiday. Passenger ships were becoming more like floating hotels. She had every amenity – superb first class suites and staterooms, shops, a beauty salon, a 300-seat cinema and a private dining room that could seat twelve as part of the main first class restaurant. She had a large cargo capacity, a garage for up to twenty-six automobiles and, after 1968, specially-fitted tanks for the transport of increasingly popular South African wines (the *S. A. Vaal* was similarly fitted with tanks for wines). The *Windsor Castle* was among the most popular British liners of the 1960s.

Dorothy Reminick recalled working in Union-Castle's London offices. 'I met a gentleman at a party in London in 1959 and who happened to be a director of the Union-Castle Line. He soon offered me a job and I became a receptionist at Rotherwick House, their grand office in London's then huge shipping business. It was a beautiful old building. I earned $35 a week in the beginning. I was soon moved to the reservations department and helped book the maiden voyage of the brand new *Windsor Castle* [in Aug 1960]. The *Pendennis Castle* had been our newest liner [1958] and had been the rage, and then we were awaiting the *Transvaal Castle* [1961]. We had lots of wealthy Brits and South Africans in first class, but lots of Africans, Indians, Anglo-Indians, half-castes and mulattoes in tourist class. In those days, you could not place a black passenger with a white passengers – and not only in staterooms, but at dining room tables. We used codes in the booking and ticketing.'

John Dimmock served for thirteen years as purser onboard the Union-Castle's flagship and largest liner, and during the final years of the famed Cape Mail Express. 'The *Windsor Castle* and the *Pendennis Castle* were our most favored big ships. We had regular passengers who came year after year – and would only sail on these two ships. It was much like a large club, a sea-going club. I especially remember one sailing wherein every first class passenger was titled. They all knew one another from previous trips and entered completely into the spirit of the voyage. These passengers would, like so many others, catch the first sailing of the New Year and later would transfer from the first class main lounge in the *Windsor* or the *Pendennis* to the main lounge of the Mount Nelson Hotel in Cape Town, which was, by the way, then owned by Union-Castle. Having escaped the dreary British winter, these passengers were affectionately known as "winter dodgers". They would return on a northbound sailing in April or May. Each year, we would rotate the first sailing in January between the *Windsor Castle* and the *Pendennis Castle*.'

'We carried lots of businessmen and government officials to and from almost all the African countries,' recalled Peter Rushton. 'Some businessmen had meetings onboard the ships. One corporate leader used to charter a whole mailship for a sort of "booze cruise" going north to England. We had a good share of holiday-makers by the 1960s, especially older people going off on garden tours in South Africa or wanting long stays in the sun at seaside resorts. We had some British migrants by the 1960s, but Australia was always the far bigger lure. All of the mail ships carried lots of cargo as well. We would have general manufactured goods going south and this included crated automobiles. On the northbound trips, we carried skins, hides, nuts, gold bullion and the mail. The gold was transported under the strictest security and offloaded at Southampton into special trains that had come down from London.'

'Our *Windsor Castle* was incredibly spacious,' remembered purser John Havers. 'She carried just over 800 passengers when other ships her size took 1,200 or even 1,400. In the early 1960s, the thirty-eight-day Christmas-New Year's roundtrip to the Cape and back in her cost some $2,500 in first class [or approximately $66 per person per day] and $900 in tourist class [approximately $23 per day].'

The late Bob Cummins served as a steward in the *Windsor Castle* and had fond memories of her. 'She was a very fine liner, which was some years ahead in design and decoration. She was incredibly spacious, which so suited her routing and the two weeks at sea. I especially recall the top suites, which were so lavish and well fitted that passengers never had to leave them. Even their meals could be served in luxurious privacy.'

'While we had six other large liners on the Cape route, the Cayzer family, which owned Union-Castle, and in particular Mr Nicholas Cayzer, thought of the *Windsor* and the *Pendennis* as floating clubs in first class,' added John Dimmock. 'They were decorated with specially woven carpets and objects d'art. Mr Cayzer would always visit these two ships when in Southampton and – with a naval architect in tow – attempt to alter, rearrange and improve the accommodation. Everything had to be in perfect condition, which of course justified the first class fares [£412 pounds for a roundtrip sailing to the Cape in 1966].'

Peter Rushton served as fourth officer aboard the *Windsor Castle* in the early 1960s and remembered, 'I sailed with Commodore Master A. G. V. Patey, who was both feared and revered. He was a towering, imposing, intimidating figure. He stood about 6 feet, 9 inches in height!' In the pursers' department, John Mengers was posted to the *Windsor Castle* in 1969. 'I recall Commodore Hort, who was a fine gentleman, but an "orders once" kind of guy.'

John Dimmock continued: 'We advanced the mailship run, increasing the schedule from 6 ½ to 7 ½ voyages per year for each ship. This was an economy move. We also noted changing trends in our passenger service. There were more and more tourists traveling with us. Our peak sailings were between January and March on the southbound trips and between April and June on the northbound runs. For the rest of the year, we began going lighter and lighter. Of course, cargo was still a very important aspect of the economics of these passenger liners. The mail was still especially important in both directions. We also carried fruits, wool, hides, gold and bulk wine from South Africa. Ironically, however, it was the cargo that would eventually spark the demise of the great Union-Castle liners.'

John Mengers recalled, 'There was serious talk of the end coming even in the late 1960s, almost ten years before the final liner voyages. Containers and containerships were the future. It was said, even hoped, however, that it would all last until 1979. But the 1973 fuel crisis killed all plans and our hope, and so the curtain came down two years earlier, in 1977. Union-Castle itself had lost interest and Safmarine container service took over. There were 100 ships in the British & Commonwealth combine in 1966. This dropped to 30–35 by 1974. By the early '80s, it was all but gone.'

'The big, six-week maritime strike in May–June 1966 was a huge blow. It was a great shock,' added Mengers. 'The unions – representing the crews and the dockers – had become too powerful and too greedy!'

'The business was winding down by 1976–77,' recollected Charles and Jean Darnell. 'The Unions dealt a death blow as well. They were increasing their demands – and becoming troublesome. We once saw the dockers deliberately drop a Jaguar into Southampton Water. They were very worried about the future. Containers had arrived and created great changes. Alone, pilferage would be cut considerably.'

By the mid-1970s, the Union-Castle liner runs were losing money. While all of the pre-Second World War liners had been retired and then there was a joint effort with the South African Marine Corporation, the Safmarine Lines, further decline was ahead. In 1975–76, the older *Edinburgh Castle* and the *S. A. Oranje*, the former *Pretoria Castle* and now in Safmarine colors, were retired and sold off to the breakers. Soon afterward, the newer, long popular *Pendennis Castle* was sold to Far Eastern buyers. By 1977, only two liners – the *Windsor Castle* and the *S. A. Vaal* (ex-*Transvaal Castle*) – remained and now sailed within a revised fleet of mostly large, high-speed containerships. Even the booking office in London's New Bond Street closed in January 1977. Later that same year, in October, the passenger runs ended completely. The *Windsor Castle* reached Southampton on her final voyage on 19 September; the *S. A. Vaal* finished hers on 10 October. In a flash, the Union-Castle UK–South African liner service of 120 years was over.

John Dimmock remembered this historic, nostalgia-filled sailing. 'There had been a rumor that the passenger mail service would continue after 1977. But the Safmarine Lines, our increasingly stronger partner, vetoed this and decided instead to invest and build more large container ships. Quite simply, containers were the future – and passengers not. Even the Cayzer family had lost interest and so the Union-Castle liner runs ended. The *Windsor Castle* was sold off to the Greek-owned Latsis Line, to become a workers' accommodation ship out in Saudi Arabia, while the *S. A. Vaal* went to the Carnival Cruise Lines of Miami, being rebuilt as the cruise ship *Festivale*. I had spent thirteen years as purser in the *Windsor Castle*. I knew most of the regular passengers and most of them knew me. There was an important, valuable sense of permanency. The final voyage wasn't a sellout, but to some loyal and sentimental passengers, the question was raised: How will we get to and from South Africa in the future?'

Harry Andrews was aboard the final sailing of the *Windsor Castle*. He recalled that voyage in September 1977: 'This was, in ways, a very nostalgically sad end of the regular ocean liner service to and from Africa. It was the end of an era – never again would there this continuous, in fact very precise convenience. The *Windsor Castle* was a fitting ship to close the service for us. She was a wonderful ship, with lovely first class accommodations. Onboard that final northbound trip, there were many nostalgic fellow passengers as well, people who had been travelling in Union-Castle liners for years and years. I also recall lots of Rhodesians being aboard, all of them returning to Britain.'

After being laid-up at Southampton in the fall of 1977 and Carnival Cruise Lines' engineers having had a look over her (after buying the *S. A. Vaal* for conversion to the Caribbean cruise ship *Festivale)*, the *Windsor Castle* was sold to Greek tanker billionaire John S. Latsis. Indeed, it has often been reported that Carnival later regretted not buying that second Castle liner for the rapidly expanding US cruise trade. The *Windsor Castle* was soon renamed *Margarita L*, in honor of John Latsis's daughter. But instead of sailing, say in the Moslem pilgrim trades in which Latsis had previous interests, she was deployed as a 'rest and recreation' ship out in Jeddah in Saudi Arabia. She returned to Greece, to lay-up in Eleusis Bay, in June 1991. There were occasional ensuing rumors, of course, that she would be revived, even as a cruise ship. Nothing came to pass, however. At the age of forty-five, she was sold to Indian scrap merchants in 2005.

The ex-*Windsor Castle* was in fact the very last of the Castle liners to go to the breakers. The final four consisted of the ex-*Kenya Castle* in 2001, the ex-*Transvaal Castle* in 2003, the ex-*Dunnottar Castle* in 2004 and finally the ex-*Windsor Castle* in 2005. Coincidentally, each ship finished its days in the same place – in far-off India, along the beaches of otherwise remote Alang.

Right: Signal Hill is in the background of this departure scene. (Albert Wilhelmi Collection)

Left: Laid-up at Freeport, Grand Bahama in 2002, with the *Rembrandt* (ex-*Rotterdam*) nested alongside. (Author's Collection)

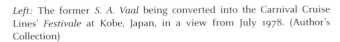

Left: The former *S. A. Vaal* being converted into the Carnival Cruise Lines' *Festivale* at Kobe, Japan, in a view from July 1978. (Author's Collection)

Below left: The restyled *Festivale*. (Author's Collection).

Below right: The *S. A. Vaal* also became the *Island Breeze*. (Andy Hernandez Collection)

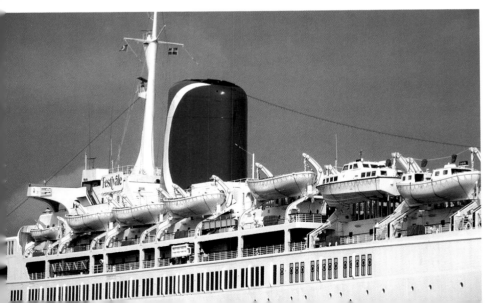

The passenger-carrying freighter *Southampton Castle*. (Luis Miguel Correia Collection)

Her sister ship, the *Good Hope Castle*. (Luis Miguel Correia Collection)

TRANSVAAL CASTLE/S. A. VAAL

John Dimmock had risen continuously within the ranks of the Union-Castle passenger fleet. As assistant purser, he served on the Round Africa service and then went to the Cape Mail run. Later, after being promoted to 2nd purser, it was back to the Round Africa ships and then to the Mail run afterward. It was set procedure at Union-Castle in those years. 'I was finally made full purser for the maiden voyage of our brand new *Transvaal Castle*, a 32,000-ton liner completed in early 1962. She was our experimental "hotel ship" with 728 total berths, all in the equivalent of cabin or second class, and with a range of accommodations from top-deck suites to economical four-berth rooms.'

Smaller than the *Windsor Castle*, the 30,212-grt *Transvaal Castle* was Union-Castle's attempt at looking at the future of ocean liner travel – an all one class setting, her 'hotel ship' designation and the introduction of female staff. She was styled more to a 'resort at sea' concept.

'The *Transvaal Castle* was a fine ship, but also a sort of "odd one out",' remembered John Mengers, who served in her pursers' department. 'She was all one-class, which made her different on the Cape Mail Run, but it was actually a sign of the times – no class distinctions. She also had lots of stewardesses and waitresses whereas the *Pendennis Castle* and *Windsor Castle* had very few women in their staff.'

Peter Rushton was aboard the final sailing of the *S. A. Vaal* in October 1977. 'The whole of Cape Town, it seemed, turned out. It was after all the end of over a century of passenger-mail service,' he remembered. 'The quaysides were mobbed. The band played *We Are Sailing*. There were tears and warships as well as fireboats providing an escort. The ship was full. There were lots of farewell parties on the thirteen-day voyage up to Southampton. I felt very sentimental and I saved all the menus. Some officers had already heard about her sale to Carnival and knew of the ship's future.'

The *S. A. Vaal* promptly found a buyer in September 1977, joining the then rather new, Miami-based Carnival Cruise Lines, today part of the world's largest cruise consortium (fourteen cruise lines and over 100 cruise ships). Renamed *Festivale*, she was sent off to the Kawasaki Shipyard in Kobe, Japan, for total rebuilding – to carry some 1,400 all-first class passengers (and no cargo whatsoever). Introduced in the following year on seven-day Caribbean cruise service from Miami, she was the largest liner to date to be used for year-round Florida-based cruising. She

Reina Del Mar in the Solent in the early 1970s. (David Williams Collection)

was sold in 1996 to Dolphin Cruise Lines, becoming the *Island Breeze*, and then changed, in 2000, to *Big Red Boat III* for Premier Cruise Lines. Laid-up at Freeport in the Bahamas after the collapse of Premier later in the fall of 2000, there were rumors that the ship might become low-income housing a minimum security prison moored in New York harbor. These ideas never came to pass and instead the ship sailed to India and the scrappers in 2003. She was broken-up just two years before her running-mate, the former *Windsor Castle*.

Above: Outbound at Southampton, the popular *Reina Del Mar.* (Luis Miguel Correia Collection)

Below: Idle at Southampton during the devastating maritime strike in May 1966. From left to right: *Good Hope Castle, Reina Del Mar* and *Edinburgh Castle.* (Union-Castle Line)

REINA DEL MAR

A very popular ship within the Union-Castle fleet, she was the only liner not built directly for the company. The 20,500-grt *Reina Del Mar* was one of the finest passenger ships built in the 1950s for British owners. Another product of the illustrious Harland & Wolff shipyard at Belfast, this three-class steamship (some 750 berths in all) was in fact an historic liner as well: she was the last British liner to serve on the long-haul route from Liverpool across the mid-Atlantic to the Caribbean, Panama Canal and the along the entire West Coast of South America. Completed in May 1956, she actually sailed for only seven years, until 1963, when the unbeatable airlines took almost all of her passengers. She had a reprieve, however – she was soon transferred to Union-Castle and refitted for a new, more profitable venue in passenger shipping: one-class cruising. She continued as a very popular cruise ship until, in the face of sharply rising fuel oil prices and operational costs, she was sold off to Taiwanese scrappers in 1975. The 601-ft long ship had barely reached twenty years of age.

'When I joined Pacific Steam Navigation Company, commonly known as PSNC, they were just retiring the twenty-eight-year-old *Reina Del Pacifico*, the predecessor to the new *Reina Del Mar*,' recalled Michael Stephen Peters, who went on to become chief engineer of the *Reina Del Mar*. 'The *Reina Del Pacifico* was soon to be retired when I first joined. She was having engine troubles in those final days and was operating on 3½ instead of 4 engines,' he added.

Peters joined the 20-knot *Reina Del Mar* in 1960–61 and had fond memories of that all-white liner that was topped-off by a single, tapered, all-yellow funnel. 'We were still doing five line voyages a year, sailing from Liverpool and then via La Rochelle, Santander and Vigo before crossing to Bermuda, Nassau, Kingston, Cartagena, the Panama Canal and then West Coast of South America ports such as Guayaquil, Callao and Valparaiso. She was a good sea boat, but you needed to understand her. Like all ships, she had her moods. For passengers, we had mostly businessmen in first class and who turned the long voyage into their holiday. We carried mostly immigrants in third class, usually from French and Spanish ports, going to South America. In January, we often had passengers who took the ten-week round voyage as a complete cruise. It was an escape from the dreary British winters. We included ports such as Tenerife, Madeira, Barbados and Curacao on these voyages.'

Like most passenger liners of that period, the *Reina Del Mar* also carried cargo as well. 'Cargo was good for extra revenue as well as ballast,' added Peters. 'We took mostly manufactured goods from Liverpool as well as specialty food items, which were destined for hotels in the Caribbean and South America. On the homeward trips, we carried tin ore and Bolivian copper as well as fish meal and cotton.'

The airlines were merciless in their competitive battle with traditional passenger ship companies like Pacific Steam Navigation. 'It was the sudden lack of passengers that killed the *Reina Del Mar*. Her demise on the South American run came quickly, in fact very quickly,' noted Michael Peters. 'Corporate thinking had changed and executives as well as staffmembers could now do a one-day flight instead of a five- of six-week voyage. And the cargo we carried was better suited to freighters. The *Reina Del Mar* was quite empty in the end, carrying less than 50 per cent of her capacity on some voyages. We experimented with one Mediterranean cruise, but cruising was not in Pacific Steam's thinking. She was soon chartered and then sold outright to the Union-Castle Line for fulltime cruising. In between, she also did some cruising for TSA, the Travel Savings Association, a bargain operation that made cruises a sort of interest on banking. I recall that, in 1964, the *Reina Del Mar* was sent over to New York for the World's Fair. The two-week trips under TSA cost as little as £60 [approx $275].'

The Travel Savings Association was formed by Max Wilson, a South African entrepeneur, in early 1963. He created a kind of banking plan – people would make planned and timed payments toward their holiday at sea while earning interest and bonuses. Advertising in the UK was very strong at first. In due course, Canadian Pacific Steamships had a 50 per cent share in this firm while Union-Castle took 25 per cent and Royal Mail Lines the final 25 per cent. Canadian Pacific's *Empress of Britain* was soon chartered (for cruising from British ports), then the *Empress of England* (for wintertime cruises from South Africa) and then the *Reina Del Mar*. Many British-flag liners were beginning to struggle in their earlier, traditional services and so TSA seemed the ideal alternate. Over 9,000 passengers were booked by mid-1963. It was all very promising, such that the three-class *Reina Del Mar* was converted to a full-time, all-one class cruise ship in 1964. It was reported that TSA would actually buy her and then run her in conjunction with the Chandris Lines' management, then an up-and-coming Greek passenger company. In the end, however, the TSA failed. Union-Castle promptly took all the shares and inherited the charter of the *Reina Del Mar* from her owners, Pacific Steam Navigation (and then technically changed to Royal Mail Lines). Union-Castle re-chartered her from 1969 onwards (until she was finally bought outright by Union-Castle in 1973).

'The TSA was shortlived. It was never as popular in Britain as it was in South Africa,' recalled John Dimmock. 'In the end, the company had high expenses, especially for advertising, and left them over-extended.'

'The *Andes* of the Royal Mail Lines was said to be very best ship in British cruising in the 1960s. She was top-drawer and catered to upper-class, even aristocratic Britain,' according to Charles and Jean Darnell. 'The *Reina Del Mar* was more of an ordinary cruise ship, sort of Union Castle-on-sea. She catered more to the working class market. Her entertainment included some professionals, but also a mix of passengers and officers.'

John Mengers recalled, 'The *Reina Del Mar* came to us mostly on charter. She was ex-Pacific Steam and later Royal Mail. Union-Castle didn't buy her until near the end. She was a strange ship in ways – she was like a rabbit warren, all up and down. She was too slow for the fast mail run – she couldn't even substitute. She could not make the necessary 22½ knots. She did have a fun onboard atmosphere, however. She didn't carry any cargo like the mail ships and so the deck officers especially loved her. We carried lots of professional people and their families on her cruises out of Southampton. In winter, she appealed to wealthy South Africans with her long voyages out of Cape Town, with some of them crossing the South Atlantic to South America and others going into the Indian Ocean.'

A sample of the *Reina Del Mar's* cruising from 1968–69 included such voyages as:

Oct 25th – Southampton, Tangier, Malta, Piraeus, Catania, Gibraltar, Southampton. 17 days from £105.
Mar 11th – Southampton, Gibraltar, Casablanca, Teneriffe, Madeira, Southampton. 12 days from £84.
Apr 3rd – Southampton to Malaga, Naples, Tunis, Alicante, Southampton. 15 days from £100.

A victim of soaring operational costs, the *Reina Del Mar* was decommissioned in April 1974 and sent off to Cornwall's River Fal to await sale. There were rumors that she might be converted to a youth hostel and moored at the Royal Albert Dock in London. Then the Greeks, Italians and even the Soviets had a look at her. But it was a tense time for fuel-hungry ocean liners. Quite prematurely, she was sold to Taiwanese shipbreakers and reached Kaohsiung on 30 July 1975. Months later, she was demolished.

Above: Idle during the 1966 strike, the *Reina del Mar* is moored alongside the *Edinburgh Castle* in a view dated 21 May. (J&C McCutcheon Collection)

Below: Another view of the *Reina del Mar* at Southampton. (J&C McCutcheon Collection)

UNION-CASTLE

Cruises by
REINA DEL MAR

PASSENGER ACCOMMODATION

Above: End of an era: the very final Mail ship sailing – the *Southampton Castle* departs from Southampton in October 1977. The Chandris Lines' *Australis* is on the right. (David Hutchings Collection)

Left: A deck plan (Andrew Kilk Collection)

The Coral Lounge aboard the *Reina Del Mar*. (Norman Knebel Collection)

The Pacific Restaurant on the *Reina Del Mar*. (Norman Knebel Collection)

Centenary Voyage aboard the chartered *Victoria*. (Author's Collection)

AFTERWORD

While reduced to pure cargo, there were no Union-Castle or even affiliate Clan Line vessels sailing by 1983. The very last ship owned by British & Commonwealth, a King Line freighter, was sold three years later, in 1986. British & Commonwealth retained a holding in Overseas Container Line until it was placed in receivership in 1990 and soon disappeared altogether. The Cayzer family interest in British & Commonwealth was sold in 1987 to John Gunn, a young tycoon, who soon sold off all the remaining assets.

In the wake of Union-Castle's passenger service, however, something of a link resumed. In 1977, with a subsidy from the British Government to continue service to St Helena and Ascension, the St Helenian Government and the Curnow Shipping Company established the St Helena Shipping Company to operate a passenger, mail and freight service between Avonmouth, the two islands and Cape Town. They soon bought the Canadian passenger-freighter *Northland Prince*, with a capacity for seventy-six passengers, for South Atlantic service as the *St Helena*. When that ship was called-up for emergency duty during the Falklands War in May 1982, however, a small freighter, the *Aragonite*, and later the Blue Funnel combination ship *Centaur* were chartered as substitutes. The *St Helena* eventually returned to service, but proved too small. A new, 6,600-grt, 140-passenger *St Helena* was built and added in 1990. She continues to date, but mostly making voyages to St Helena and Ascension only from Cape Town.

Safmarine Lines actually hoped to reopen something of a liner service between Cape Town and Southampton in 1984. They purchased the 500-bed German cruise ship *Astor*. A few 'line voyages' followed but proved unsuccessful, even disappointing. The ship itself was unsuited to the long voyages and there were too few passengers. In harsh reality, the old guard of Union-Castle was gone. Passenger loads consisted now of budget South African tourists and students. The ship soon turned to fulltime cruising. A second, almost identical *Astor* was built in 1987, but her mainstay was year-round cruises. In 1990, Safmarine began offering ten passenger berths on four of its large, 55,000-grt container ships sailing between Southampton and the Cape. Well served and popular, passenger service was not continued, however, when the new containerships were built a decade later.